ELEMENTS OF
TEACHING IN KINDERGARTEN

ELEMENTS OF TEACHING IN KINDERGARTEN

Edited by

M. Husain

ANMOL PUBLICATIONS PVT. LTD.

NEW DELHI - 110 002 (INDIA)

ANMOL PUBLICATIONS PVT. LTD.
H.O.: 4374/4B, Ansari Road, Daryaganj,
New Delhi-110 002 (India)
Ph.: 23278000, 23261597
B.O.: No. 1015, Ist Main Road, BSK IIIrd Stage
IIIrd Phase, IIIrd Block,
Bangalore - 560 085 (India)
Visit us at: www.anmolpublications.com

Elements of Teaching in Kindergarten

PRINTED IN INDIA

Printed at Mehra Offset Press, Delhi.

Contents

Preface

'Elementary education' is much debated universal issue, which is given emphasis as a fundamental right of each and every human being. All the nation-states the world over have made statutory provisions to ensure that none could be deprived of elementary education. Many world organisations are playing vital role in advancing the status of elementary education. Despite all these measures a large number of children in different parts of the world are still deprived of basic education.

This work in three volumes intends to focus on some vital issues pertaining to the theme. Attempts are made to gather the well researched material, based on the empirical findings of different scholars of repute from various settings.

As the information is drawn from various authoritative sources, no claim is of originality. We are deeply beholden to all those whose works and views are cited or substantially borrowed herein for making the work comprchensive and more useful. Besides these, we are grateful to one and all who have rendered the assistance while executing the plan of the work. Finally Mr. J.L. Kumar, Managing Director, Anmol Publications Pvt. Ltd. deserve all appreciation for undertaking the publication of this venture.

—**Editor**

1
The Kindergarten Education: A View

"Come, let us live with our children!"

This appeal, uniting and comprising all, also expresses all our feelings, all our thoughts today, at the conclusion of the old and the beginning of the new year. We indeed anticipate, hope, and believe that it is the more or less clear feeling, the uttered or silent thought of many—of all, indeed, who lead considerate and thoughtful lives. Therefore, even to-day in the old year, the determination to "live with our children," and the immediate realization of this determination, express the desire felt by many for union in spirit and for common effort; consequently the coming year from its first day, even from its first hour, may thus become the most important opportunity for humanity—an opportunity to unite for the welfare of the individual human being as well as for the good of all humanity. Such united effort will make this indeed a *new* year.

But what awakes in us the anticipation, what secures to us the belief and gives us the conviction that the idea, "Come, let us live with our children," is not only to-day in the old, the departing, and in the new, the coming year, but at all times, the uniting, fundamental, living thought of many; and that it not only finds accord and sympathy in the human breast, but is held fast in the life and deeds of humanity?

There is no man who was not a child—not one who does not know at his stage of culture what he became or did not become by the holding fast or not holding fast to this living thought; yet all feel deeply, and, indeed, express frequently to themselves and others, what they might have become by a general adherence to this idea. If we ponder even for a short time on the definite holding fast to this idea, we must deeply experience and clearly recognize that by carrying it out ourselves, by the remembrances of our childhood which it arouses in us, by the complementing and completing which it gives to our own life, and by the demand which it makes and the opportunity which it gives for our own increasing improvement, we live our own best life.

This cry escapes us; it hopes to find sympathy and accord in the breast of man; the all-embracing heart, the penetrating intellect, perceive it in all things as a silent feeling, a quiet thought, and so as the thought of the world.

Heart and mind see it express itself indeed and as a fact in the whole of which man is only a part, of which he himself is a member. Does not the sun with all the stars say it to the earth with all its creatures, all its children? Do not the elements, earth, water, air, light, heat, say it to one another in reference to all forms of earth? Do not all the parts of every plant say it to one another in reference to the seed quietly growing in its place? Yes, in all Nature, where life and activity make themselves known, where the individual strives to absorb the unit and the whole (as, for example, the kernel contains the nature of the whole tree) in order to make it more perfectly known and demonstrated in manifoldness and totality—everywhere we see the idea, "Come, let us live with our children," express itself as the maxim which applies to all life.

Should not now the conscious human being destined to rise to yet higher consciousness, express aloud for mutual advancement and recognition, and also for common employment and accomplishment, what nature already silently express as a general law, a prevailing demand of life?

Therefore, this appeal hopes to reach those who will not only sympathize with it, but also assent to it and respond to it in action. For is not man more than every other creature in nature, and the child more than the germ of a plant? The tree germ bears within itself the nature of the whole tree, the human being bears in himself the nature of all humanity; and is not, therefore, humanity born anew in each child? But who has fathomed this nature? Who has measured it? Does it not rest in God?

Thus the appeal, "Come, let us live with our children," is a true life call, uniting all in itself as in a central point, on the dividing line between the departing and the coming year; since it indeed mingles with all life; not only uniting human beings and human life with each other and with humanity, not only uniting the creature with the universe, but even with the fountain of all life, with the Creator, who said, "Let us make man in our own image."

Therefore, "Come, let us live with our children!"

The Deed

Where true resolution and genuine effort for comprehensive representation of life exist there appears also directly the deed, as is, in general, the case with the clear, self-dependent, uniting thought that immediately seeks also to manifest itself in action. The fundamental and living thought of humanity, "Come, let us live with our children," becomes, when manifested in action, *an institution* for fostering family life and for the cultivation of the life of the nation, and of mankind, through fostering the impulse to activity, investigation, and culture in man, in the child as a member of the family, of the nation, and of humanity; *an institution* for self-instruction, self-education, and self-cultivation of mankind, as well as for all-sided and therefore for individual cultivation of the same through play, creative self-activity, and spontaneous self-instruction; first of all, for families and schools for the nature of little children; for primary and public schools as well as for every person who strives for completeness and unity in his culture; to the carrying out of which the spirit of this reciprocal appeals has united many families in Germany, Switzerland, and North America.

Foundation of the Whole

The development and formation of the whole future life of each being is contained in the beginning of its existence. The untroubled realization and the undiminished efficiency of the life of each being depend wholly on the comprehension and fostering, on the recognition and firm carrying out of this beginning.

Man, as a child, resembles the flower on the plant, the blossom on the tree; as these are in relation to the tree, so is the child in relation to humanity—a young bud, a fresh blossom; and as such, it bears, includes, and proclaims the ceaseless reappearance of new human life.

As the flower bud of the tree—connected with twig, branch, and trunk, with the whole ramification of root and crown, and, through this double ramification, with earth and heaven—stands in united coherence and reciprocal exchange with the whole universe for the development and vivification of its being, so stands man also, in all-sided developing life-exchange with nature, with humanity, and with all spiritual efforts and influences—with the universal life.

The blissful development of the human being which leads to perfection and completion, and the fitting him for the attainment of his destiny, and thus for the attainment by effort of the genuine joy and true peace of life, depend alone on the correct comprehension of man, even as a child, in respect to his nature as well as to his relations, and on the corresponding treatment of man in accordance with this nature and these relations.

But man is a created being, and, as such, is at the same time a part and a whole (therefore, a part-whole), for, on the one side, he is, as a creation, a part of the universe; but, on the other side, he is also a whole, since—just because he is a creature—the nature of his Creator (a living and creating nature full of life, and testifying to life, therefore in itself single) lives in him.

This original and fundamental nature of man, as being life in itself and therefore again giving life, makes itself known in man's impulse to creative formation. This fundamental nature makes itself known even in the child by the instinct for observing, analyzing, and again uniting—that is, by the instinct for formative and creative activity. Indeed, the fostering of this instinct in the child makes manifest the life of man, at the same time wholly satisfying the demands of that life.

Man, as a child, appears to be conditioned and mediates by the father and mother.

Father, mother, and child form a triune life-whole—a family. The child creates the family and the family-life by its advent; and, on the other hand, man's continuous presence on earth is indispensably linked with the family. The family and child reciprocally condition each other; neither exists without the other; they form in themselves an inseparable unit.

As in his original advent in the universe (on the earth), so also in the family man again makes his appearance as a true part-whole, since he is a whole in himself, and also, at the same time, a necessary member of the family life-whole.

Only as a member of the family will it be possible for man to become a symmetrical, real, whole man; indeed, the family as a whole is a real, whole, human existence, and the family life as a whole is real, complete, human life.

As now the family is the fundamental condition of the production of man and the mediator of his existence, so also man as a child attains fully the development of his instinct for creative self-activity only when connected with and conditioned by the family; then only is it possible for him to live in complete accordance with this instinct.

All genuine human education and true human training, and so also this endeavor of ours, are linked with the quiet fostering in the family of this instinct for activity, with the thoughtful development of the child for the satisfaction of this instinct, and with the fitting of the child to be active in conformity with it.

It is the aim of our endeavor to make it possible for man freely and spontaneously to develop, to educate himself from his first advent on earth, as a whole human being, as a whole in himself, and in harmony and union with the life-whole—to make it possible for him to inform and instruct himself, to recognize himself thus as a definite member of the all-life, and, as such, freely and spontaneously to make himself known—freely and spontaneously to live.

Moreover, the first and fundamental appearance of love—of the love of parents and child, the family-love—is found now in the family-life; indeed, the family is love itself become personal. The parental love manifest itself in its whole nature just in and by means of the nourishing and developing of the child's impulse to creative activity, and in the supplying of the means for this development. The fostering of this impulse arouses and strengthens the love of brothers and sisters. This fostering of the impulse to creative activity is thus a comprehensive expression of true love of parents and child, of the genuine family-love, and so reveals, and at the same time wholly satisfies, all love and the nature of love.

Considering man as a created being, it is also quite indispensable to regard and treat him, even in childhood as well as through his whole life, as a creative being, and to train and prepare him so that, while himself creating, he may, even from his earliest years, find and recognize the Creator, the creation, and the created, and may thus find and recognize himself in this threefold relation and connection according to the measure of his increasing capacity. So trained, he will be enabled to understand and comprehend, and thus to attain to that which is man's calling and destiny as an earthly being—namely, to recognize God in the creation and in the creature, and therefore in man; to recognize himself in himself and in mankind; and thus each in the others, and the others in each individual: to promote this recognition, to represent it and to make it representable, to perceive it and to make it perceptible.

But to see, to recognize, and to perceive, require and presuppose light and almost are light. Recognition therefore develops light in and around the human being, from the satisfying fostering of his impulse to creative and observant activity. The destiny and calling of man (to be light and to move in light), as well as the possibility for him by the fostering of the impulse to creative activity to fulfil the above-mentioned destiny, is thus shown to us.

As we now see man, even from his first appearance upon the earth and his first entrance into the family, move in a threefold way, which is yet single in itself (therefore a triune way), in and by means of life, in and by means of love, in light and by means of light—in his seeing, perceiving, recognizing, and remembering—we also see that the careful fostering of his impulse to creative activity completely corresponds to and satisfies this triune life of man. But this triune way in which man moves is, above all comparison, important to the human being; for God shows himself in Nature, in the universe, as life; God reveals himself in humanity as love (and in love); and God manifests himself in wisdom (in the spirit) as light and in light. So God is the life, the love, and the light; and in such a triune way he appears as the Creator and in the creature.

In life, love, and light, and as life, love, and light therefore, the being and Nature of the child, of the man, are made known as existing, are revealed as having been realized and as still realizing.

By life, the child appears predominantly connected with Nature, with the all; by love, he appears pre-eminently united with humanity; and by light, he appears to be one with wisdom, with God.

Man as a created being is thus in his first period of life on earth to be regarded, considered, and fostered in the all-sidedness of his relations as a threefold child, as it were; or, as a child in three separate relations which are united in themselves—as a child of Nature, as a human child, and as a child of God; that is, first, according to his common, earthly, and natural condition and connection, according to his life; then, according to his special human existence, to his love; finally, according to his original spiritual nature, his anticipations and perceptions, his remembrance, recognitions, and intentions, his knowledge and his wisdom. In his first relation (as a child of Nature) man is to be considered as a being bound, chained, unconscious, subject to impulses, sentient, living only corporeally; in the latter relation, as a child of God, as a free being not only fitted for consciousness, destined to consciousness, but already in anticipation conscious of his nature, therefore following by his own will a high and genuine unity of life as a thoughtful, perceptive, intuitive, spiritual, knowing, and wise being; and in the intermediate relation (as a child of humanity) as a being struggling from bondage and chains toward freedom; from singleness toward union, toward consciousness; from separation toward union, toward peace; an aspiring being devoted constantly to the above-named efforts; and, in the anticipation of finding unity, a joyously living being.

To become clearly conscious of all the conditions and relations in which and by means of which man exists, and to faithfully live up to the requirements of these conditions and relations, make man (as a presence) first become man in consciousness and action; and make it possible for him to become a whole, complete human being by leading him to an equally careful and joyous fulfilment of each of his duties, and by making it possible for him to fulfill the totality of the duties of man in harmony.

Only if the child, the human being, be comprehended and treated through the whole fostering of the impulse of his life (his impulse to creative activity), in the triunity of his nature, as living, loving, and perceiving, in the unity of his life, in the all-sidedness of his circumstances and relations; if he be comprehended and treated as an earthly being in accordance with what he is, what he has, and what he will become; only if he comprehends the outer world around him in like triunity (and thus recognizes the revelation of the divine in like triunity) in its unity, in each individual, and in the sum of all unities—only thus can man develop himself as that which he is, as the manifold and articulated (but in himself single) whole, and, at the same time, a member of the great whole—of all life; only thus can he develop himself in conformity with his destiny, and be faithful to his vocation. He will thus form an entirely and a unity of life from and around himself, and, in and by means of his creative life, God, Nature, and humanity will reveal themselves in unity and singleness. Man himself will make them known as they reveal themselves to him in and for the all-sided union, the genuine peace, and the true joy of life.

So, founded on the nature of man and on his instinct for formation and activity, and connected with the fostering of this impulse, the aim of this institution is to be a living whole, or, as it were, a tree in itself, as well as to provide means of employment, and consequently of culture and instruction, founded on the relations of man to Nature and life; means, which when applied in a lively manner to the child from the first stage of its spiritual awakening and of its use of limbs and senses, and constantly advancing with the growth of its powers, develop it on all sides, and therefore in union with itself, with Nature, and with the laws of life. Thus, this institution aims to establish means of employment and so of cultivation and teaching, which, as they shows the objects of cultivation and instruction in union with each other, at the same time represent them in harmony and accord with the development of Nature and of man, and satisfy the requirements of both.

2

The First Action of Child

As the newborn child, like a ripe kernel of seed corn dropped from the mother plant, has life in itself, and, also like the kernel, develops life from itself in progressive but increasingly spiritual coherence with the common life-whole by its own spontaneous action, so activity and action are also the first phenomena of awakening child-life. This activity and this action are, indeed, the actual expression of the internal and innermost through and by the outward, therefore inward activity devoted to observing and working with the external, to overcoming outward hindrances merely as such, and to penetrating the external. Hence early in the life of the child appears an activity in harmony with feeling and perception, indicating a slumbering apprehension and comprehension of itself by the child as well as an already germinating individual capacity.

The nature of man as a being destined to become, and in future to be, conscious of personality, although at first apparent only in slight outlines, yet already stamped with sufficient distinctness to be observed and comprehended—lies in the quite peculiar character of childish activity even when the so-called three months' slumber has just ended; in the totality of the first childish action (especially after this time), a totality which can not be more fittingly designated than by the expression "to busy one's self"; in the impulse of the child to employ itself, an impulse awakening at the same time with the inner life of the child—that is, in the impulse (in accord with feeling and perception) to be active for the increasing development of its own life; and, as we remarked in the beginning, man, even from babyhood, in his triune relation to Nature, to humanity, and to God, finds his needs completely satisfied by the correct comprehension and by the right fostering of his impulse to busy himself, by the care and oversight of childish occupations.

We are repeatedly impressed with the conviction that everything which is to be done for the true human development of the child, and all efforts which are to be made for such an education as will satisfy the needs of all sides of its being, must be connected with, and proceed from, the fostering of the impulse to employment, and the oversight of the first employment of the child. For the impulse to employment corresponds to the triune activity of man in doing, experiencing, and thinking. This impulse corresponds fully to his nature, which is to have power to perceive, to comprehend, to obtain self-knowledge, to become more and more conscious of his own personality, and to become spontaneous. Therefore the whole human bringing, all humanity in the child, and life itself, is comprehended by means of the impulse to employment.

Notwithstanding the existence of the impulse to employment which manifests itself early in the life of the human being (though but the slightest traces of it are at first perceptible), it has been commonly stated, but from a quite incorrect point of view, that the child is so helpless when born, and develops to self-dependence so slowly, as to require the mother's fostering and help for a long time; it has even been said that man is in this respect behind and below the animals. Only, as we shall yet more often see in the future, just exactly *that* with which human nature is charged as a necessary consequence of the existence of human beings upon earth, or which is at least alleged as a speaking evidence of the great imperfection of man, constitutes his evident superiority over the other creatures on earth, is a sign of his dignity, and an assertion that man is created in the image of God, so that he may recognize and demonstrate his likeness to God—that is, that He has appeared upon earth, and under earthly limitations for that purpose. For we recognize through this helplessness that man is destined to free, self-active progress, and is called to higher and higher stages of consciousness of self.

The animal, whose life-impulses, powers, and qualities, whose instincts, as they are called, are at birth so definite and strong that it, on the contrary, does not fail, and indeed in a free natural condition can not fail, to overcome by those instincts every obstacle in each department of its life, the animal, just on account of its strong instincts, can not arrive at the knowledge of its powers, its qualities, its nature, its unity, and therefore can not arrive at a recognition of its manifoldness, nor, above all, at the anticipation and recognition of unity as such; still less can it give to itself an account thereof, for it lacks all points of comparison. It lacks the points of companion which (as is the case with man) proceed from their to that even the weakest manifestations of power meet in their workings with obstructions which even increase as the power itself increases, and will thus with difficulty be overcome, or prevailed over and annihilated.

It is, as already stated, quite different with the life of man, in which at first scarce anything can be easily accomplished without extraneous help, and consequently nothing without hindrances, but especially nothing through the superiority of power from within (such, for example, as the just-hatched duckling shows on the water); thus everything external is to be overcome, even though there be a preponderance of helplessness, through the inner enhancing and outward strengthening and increasing of power by the free activity of the will. This inner self-enhancing of power, proceeding from spontaneous of the will and outward strengthening and increasing of this power, effected by this inner self-enhancing, constitute the superiority of man over the animal, and this so much the more as man is born in the most extreme condition of helplessness.

The helplessness of the newborn human being in respect to everything external is the opposite of his future ability for self-helpfulness (an ability which is in unison with the unity and the wholeness of life) through the enhancement of his will power and consequently his power of action. As now outward helplessness is the opposite of possible enhancement of inward power, so the latter is to be aroused and become recognized and strengthened by the former. As, in general, everything is and will be best recognized by means of that which is its opposite, therefore helplessness is to be overcome by the enhancement of power; for it is just the conquering, or rather the prevailing over and so annihilating the outward hindrance of life by one's own will power and one's own enhanced power of action, which preserves to man peace, joy, and freedom in his own consciousness, and thus elevates him to that likeness to God for which he is destined. Helplessness and personal will (one's own will), therefore, soon become the two hinges, the opposite turning points (poles) of the child's life, of which the middle point and point of union, and thus the balance point, is independent activity and free activity, self-occupation and self-employment. Herein lies for the educator and fosterer of the human being the key to the inner and outer life of man in childhood and youth, and to the phenomena of this inner and outer life, often as difficult to explain as to treat and to adjust. By means of this key there is opened to the educator an unobstructed view of the lights and shadows of child-life and of its phenomena, which so often seem to contradict one another. From the impulse to activity and from spontaneous employment of one's self, or rather from the three (helplessness, one's own will, and employment of one's self), soon proceed habitude and custom (often indolence and a tendency to seek one's own ease). This fact is as remarkable and worthy of notice as it is easily recognizable, as each phenomenon—which is especially to be considered in the life of children and in the correct estimation of that life—calls forth its opposite. One willingly makes one's self at home where one can act freely; and, on the other hand, one can act freely where one has made one's self at home.

It is therefore just as important for the child that those who have it in charge should notice its customs, its habits, and to what it accustoms itself, especially in respect to cause and effect, as that they should notice and foster its impulse to activity. Indeed, one can see clearly that just this trait of the child of accustoming and inuring itself to something, and of growing together with its surroundings and becoming one with them, proves the early existence of the impulse to activity and employment even when the child outwardly appears inactive (passive); since the child accommodates itself to outward surroundings, relations, and requirements, in order thus to obtain more space for the play of its inner activity.

As now habit in the child proceeds from spontaneous and independent activity, so also imitation springs from it; and it is no less important for the fostering of childhood and child-life and for observing it to keep this origin of imitation in view than to keep in view the phenomena of habitude, custom, and independent activity. For we see the whole inner spiritual life of the child manifest the threefold phenomenon, spontaneous activity, habit, and imitation, as a triune phenomenon. These three phases are intimately united early in the life of the child, and give us the most important discoveries concerning child-life in respect to foundation and result, and the surest indices for the early correct treatment of the child. None of these phenomena should therefore be excluded from a comprehensive study of children, such as would satisfy the nature of the human being, for all three are alike deeply grounded in human nature in respect to their source. The three activities taken together also disclose the following aims, which wholly correspond to the nature of the child as a human being. These aims are, to keep itself such as it feels and finds itself—a being which is independent and yet supported by the whole; to strengthen, exercise, and develop its limbs and senses, and to make them free, thus within itself and by its own efforts to attain more and more independence and personality, and to reveal itself in its personality; finally, to obtain knowledge of the independence and personality—that is, of the independent existence—of that which surrounds it, and to convince itself of that existence.

This joint aim of life, the joint activity proceeding from it and the unity of life at the foundation of both, are expressed by the child's first quiet fixing of its eyes. Hence the child's first clear gaze so delight and uplifts those who witness it, for the child thereby proclaims self-dependence and personality in itself and his ability to maintain these qualities; it also acknowledges the self-dependence and personality of these around it and anticipates the future (though as yet deeply slumbering) unity of life; it therefore announces the elevation of man above unconscious nature, and fully expresses his dignity, his humanity.

Therefore, the first voluntary employments of the child, if its bodily needs are satisfied and it feels well and strong, are observation of its surroundings, spontaneous reception of the outer world, and play, which is independent outward expression of inward action and life. This dual expression, taking in and carrying out in life, is necessarily grounded in the nature of the child as well as of the human being in general, since its first earthly destiny is to attain by critical reception of the outer world into itself, by manifold inward impressions and through outward realization of its inner world, and by critical comparison of both, to the recognition of their unity, to the recognition of life as such, and to faithful living in accordance with the requirements of life.

Since we now see man at an early age comprehend his destiny by means of these three activities, so the collective phenomena of his whole future life find their solution in these activities, which form, as it were, the triune point of reference and vital point thereof.

That he may fulfill and attain his destiny, man is endowed on the one hand with senses, the organs by which he can make the external internal; on the other hand with bodily strength and limbs, by which he can represent his inner nature outwardly, therefore always by material means; finally, that he may comprehend spiritual unity, the nature of man appears as an anticipating and individual soul, because this nature is in itself a perceptive and uniting spirit.

It is therefore evident how important the training of body and senses is for man even in the early stages of his existence; and, from the more spiritual, comparing, and uniting point of view, it is also evident how important the *kind* of observation of the outer world and its reception into the inner nature of man, and also the *kind* of the voluntary, playful occupations of the child, are for the method of experience as to its conclusions and reasons, for the spirit of the knowledge and insight which it draws therefrom, and so for the expression of its nature, which makes itself known thereby.

For, as the life of man in all the necessary variety of its phenomena is in itself a complete unity, one can recognize and consider even in the first baby life, though only in their slightest traces and most delicate germs, all the spiritual activities which in later life become predominant.

Beloved parents and nurses, do not say, "How could the last-named spiritual tendencies be contained in the life of the little child, which appears as yet so unconscious and helpless?" If they were not contained in the little child they could not be developed at all from it; but on the fact that they are contained therein based the love for children of the greatest friend of children, his judgment concerning them, his placing them on the same plane with himself, and his demands for them. Were these directions and references not contained in the child's nature, the quickly discerning sense of the mother would not treat the child from the first moment of its existence as an understanding, perceptive and capable being, and so these directions and references could never become the fruit of its life; for where there is not the germ of something, that something can never be called forth and appear.

The outermost point and innermost ground of all phenomena of the earliest life and activity of the child is this: the child must bring into exercise the dim anticipation of conscious life in itself as well as of life around it; and consequently must exercise power, test and thus compare power, exercise independence, and test and thus compare the degree of independence.

Therefore, as soon as the life of the child, its power of spontaneous and voluntary action and its use of limbs and senses are aroused; when it can freely move its little arms and hands, when it can perceive and distinguish tones, and can turn its attention and its gaze in the direction from which these tones come; let us give to the child for its spontaneous and voluntary action an object which expresses stability and yet movability, which in this stability and movability can be grasped and handled by the child; in which, as in its own mind, the unity of all manifoldness is contained; which it perceives in its formal existence, in which, therefore, though as yet quite unconsciously, it can see its own self-dependent, stable and yet movable life, as it were, in a mirror, as well as test and exercise such life by such an object. And this plaything is the *sphere*, or rather the *ball*.

3

Institution for Children's Creative Activity

Because all life rests in one unity, and because all existing life wells forth from this unity, he who will work benevolently and fruitfully, blissfully and constantly, progressively developing to increasing perfection, must try to act and to live in inner united coherence with the development of Nature and man, with the stage of cultivation of the understanding and of the use of the reason now attained, thus in full accord with the present stage of development of Nature and humanity (that is, of the whole universe), as well as in pure harmony with the inner demands and the stage of development of the individual or whole.

Thus, he who desires to work helpfully and fruitfully, constantly and beneficially, for the welfare and founding of the family, must, in harmony with the stage of development of his family and its members, connect his efforts with a comprehensive and unital, a simple and yet general human fundamental ideas, at least with such a general perception of life; or, rather, he must make such a perception his starting point. He who does not this just in proportion as he does not do so builds on quicksand.

Now such ideas, which must lie at the foundation of the human influence, especially of the educating influence as a human one, have been already definitely and clearly expressed above; it will wholly suffice to the present aim—the demonstration of the plan of the before mentioned institution—to deduce the necessity and nature of the institution in view from a principle derived from experience, a principle which rests in and is explained by one of the highest, final, fundamental ideas, and whose innermost coherence with the highest thought of life comes out definitely enough for this aim.

This principle derived from experience is:

The present effort of mankind in harmony with the phenomena in Nature and the time, with the collective all-life, is an endeavor after freer self-development, after freer self-formation, and freer determining of one's own destiny. In fact, the more or less conscious aim of those who make thus effort to find out the unity of the individual and the manifold, the inner coherence of the separate, the accord of the opposite, the abiding with the changing, the true being behind the phenomenal, and the spirit in the form.

Therefore, the more or less clear aim of the individual is to attain clearness about himself and about life in its unity, its foundation, as well as in its thousand ramifications and in its relations to completeness and unity of life, to comprehension and right use of life, according to recognition and insight, as well as to representation and accomplishment; and all this by voluntary choice, by spontaneous and personal activity, and in accord with all.

This portrays the present degree of development of mankind in character. Therefore, if we would not annihilate our children spiritually and bodily, if we would not cripple their present childish life, the youthful life next to be attained by them, their future life as citizens, their future domestic life, and their whole life as members of humanity, we must in the education and training of our children be faithful to the requirements of their individual nature, as well as in accord and coherence with the present stage of human development, which is conditioned by and proceeds from the development of the whole world, the collective all-life.

That this highest aim of life may be attained, the present time makes upon education and the educator, parents and nurses, the following wholly indispensable requirement—to comprehend the earliest activity, the first action of the child, the impulse to formation and to spontaneous and personal activity (the first manifestations of which appear at an early age), to encourage the earliest employment of children at home, the impulse to self-culture and self-instruction through self-shaping, self-observation, and self-testing.

Every one who observes with any attention even the first stage of child-life is met therein (frequently as well as definitely) by the requirement of fostering the child's impulse to activity, but he is also met by the perception of how little is done to satisfy the requirement generally, but especially how little is done to satisfy it in a judicious way—that is, in accord with the nature of man.

Very many loyal parents and members of the family, very many anxious fathers and grandfathers, loving mothers and grandmothers, cousin and uncles, fostering elder brother and sisters, and sympathizing family friends and friends of the children, are indeed inclined carefully and suitably to nourish and foster the impulse of childhood and youth to acquire information spontaneously by self-activity, but, on the one hand, only too often the requisite, wholly suitable means, and, indeed, the needed capacity and dexterity, knowledge, and training are lacking; but on the other hand, also, the child's employments as well as the means and objects of such employment (the plays and the playthings) are too little—indeed, not at all—recognized in their true, deep significance, are too little comprehended in their general human interest and spirit, which, just because they are general and human, continue to cultivate the man already grown up and rich in knowledge, and are too little presented in their connection with life in general. The consequence of this is, that these means of play offer too little—indeed, nothing at all—to the adult for the nourishment and continued development of his or her own life; hence, aside from the duty of older people to children, it seems to the adult a waste of time to employ himself or herself with fostering the child's impulse to activity by means of and in its plays.

Now the aim of this institution is to make the needs and requirements of the child-world—needs and requirements to which we have just referred—correspond to the present stage of development of humanity, and to provide for parents and adults who find themselves in the just-mentioned position in regard to the fostering of the children intrusted to them, appropriate plays and means of employment, and consequently of instruction and cultivation—of education in general—and, above all, means adapted to the mind, spirit, and life of the child; therefore to be able to prove the equally necessary, natural, and human reciprocal call of the families, "Come, let us live with our children," to be as general as it is rich in blessing. Hence the plan of this institution is as follows:

Plan

I. To provide plays and means of employment (consequently of culture) which satisfy the needs alike of parents and child, of age and youth, of educator and pupil; which therefore nourish and strengthen, develop and form the life of the children, as well as promote the life of the parents and adults—or at least afford them spiritual and intellectual nourishment while they employ themselves in playing with the children—indeed, we might say even while they, as experienced and intelligent parents, and observant and clear-sighted older people, merely observe the plays and spontaneous employment of these children in a thoughtful manner—that is, with spiritual and intellectual sympathy.

The spirit and character of these means of employment, and so of instruction, are therefore that—

1. They proceed from unity, and develop in all manifoldness from unity in accordance with the laws of life. They begin with the simplest, and, at each particular stage, again begin with that which is relatively the simplest; but afterward advance in reciprocally beneficial relation to one another, and according to the necessary laws contained in the nature of the things themselves, from the simplest to the most

complex, from that which is as yet undeveloped to that which is fully grown, and so on in accord with natural and spiritual development—in general, with the development of life.

2. The aim of each of the means of employment, and likewise of education, is purely human instruction and cultivation—that is, such as is in itself single as well as unifying—so that through the right, judicious, and spirited use of each (even of the smallest) of these means the human being both in childhood and in maturity will be advanced educated, and formed as an individual, and also comprehended and developed as a member of humanity—therefore as a member of his family, of his nation, and of humanity, and also as a member of Nature and of the universe—of the one-life and the all-life.

3. The totality of the plays and means of employment, which are at the same time means of formation of character and of education, as it proceeds from a single, fundamental principle of culture observable in Nature, authenticated by history, and proving itself to be purely human, forms a stable, coherent whole, all the parts of which reciprocally explain and mutually benefit one another. This whole, therefore, resembles a tree with its many branches.

4. Each individual thing which is attained, however small and simple, or however large and complex it may be, is therefore always a self-contained whole, and so resembles a bud, or a kernel of corn, from which manifold new developments can be called forth, which again converge into a higher unity. Wherefore he who judiciously, energetically, and carefully uses for his little charge what is attained, is himself manifoldly develop as well as harmoniously cultivated.

5. These means of employment will, in the course of their presentation, embraces the whole province of general and fundamental instruction of the faculties of perception. They also will embrace the groundwork of all future extended instruction as a whole, and are founded on the nature of man as an existent, living, and perceptive being. But, as the child at first feels and finds himself in space, and finds others

occupying the space around him, these means of employment proceed from space, from the observation of space and from the knowledge which comes from that observation, going on by means of the development and training of the limbs and senses of the human being, and by means of language to comprehend Nature in its most essential directions; so that finally man, who at first could find himself only in space and by means of space, may now learn to find himself as an existent, living, feeling and thinking, understanding and intelligent, perceptive and rational being, to retain the perception of himself as such a being, and, as such, to strive to live.

6. It is quite essential to the spirit and character of these means of fostering independent action in the child that they should lead to the thoughtful observation of Nature and of life in all its parts and phenomena; but it is also essential that they should lead to the anticipation and recognition, and finally to the comprehension of the inner coherence of material things, and of the phenomena of life, and also of the oneness of the material and spiritual worlds, and the increasing similarity of their laws.

7. Thinking and discriminating parents will therefore find these plays and this playing of use and benefit in their business or calling, whether it be an inner one devoted to knowledge or an outward one devoted to work, the results of which can be seen, as even the occupying of one's self therewith in the circle of the children is invigorating and beneficial, elevating and purifying, in its retroactive effect on the life of the adult.

8. Each play, each means of employment, and each means of self-teaching will be accompanied by sufficing instructions which embrace the subject on all sides. These instructions will contain—

a. Description of the nature of play and its higher references to man and to life.

b. Statements of the relation of each individual play and means of employment to the totality, so that with each is specified what, in general, precedes it, what accompanies it, and what follows it; therefore, on what it is founded, and of what it is itself the foundation.

c. A direction sufficient to enable parents and nurses and teachers to use the play, the thing being vivified by the word, the word illustrated by drawings, and these again explained by the word and the thing itself.

d. These instructions will especially render prominent the laws of mental growth proceeding from and leading to the use of play and to its different representations.

e. Will especially state the firmly, beautifully, and clearly formed truths of Nature and life obviously contained therein, for the purpose of self-discovery, self-observation, and further self-development, in order to unite man more and more in and with himself, as well as with Nature and life, with the unity and fount of life.

II. In the gradual accomplishment of the whole course, such means of self-cultivation and self-instruction are to be provided as satisfy the needs and requirements of the present stage of human development, and also suffice for adults who wish to continue their own cultivation in accordance therewith. Here will be presented, in conformity with each line of culture and instruction, comprehensive summaries of all parts which belong together, and of the relatively higher unities and the highest unity of these parts. The purpose of these summaries is that the human being—as all unity is, properly speaking, invisible, and only perceptible in the innermost—may be led from the visible and external to the invisible and internal, from the appearance to the true being, and, thus led into himself, may also be led to God; thus man may be clearly shown to man in his nature, in his unfolding, and in his relation to totality and to unity—to Nature and to God—and so may come to man, in all the relations of life, unity and clearness, consciousness and penetration in cultivation, as well as in life and in insight, and therefore joyousness, peace, and freedom.

Since we are now deeply convinced that man, even though only unconsciously faithful to his nature and to the higher and highest demands of humanity of which he is a member, seeks to learn to comprehend and present the outer as well as the inner coherence of life in the higher and highest living unity—in spite of the actual and undeniably apparent disjointedness in life, and the generally prevailing seeking merely for that which is directly and immediately useful in the striving for information—we hope by means of this institution to answer to a need in accordance with the spirit to the age, and to provide such an education of childhood as will correspond to the deepest and most secret (even unknown to themselves) wishes and yearnings of parents and adults, as fosterers of children.

The course of plays and means of employment is to begin with that which is simplest and near; for only that which proceeds from the simplest, smallest, and near can develop from and explain by itself the manifold, great, and distant—can show the spirit of unity; and it is only the single spirit which creates the single life.

And thus we show here, for the fostering of the impulse to activity and of the creative nature of the child.

4

First Plaything of Childhood: The Ball

Even the word 'ball', in our significant language, is full of expression and meaning, pointing out that the ball is, as it were, an image of the all (*der B-all ist ein Bild des All*); but the ball itself has such an extraordinary charm, such a constant attraction for early childhood, as well as for later youth, that it is beyond comparison the first as well as the most important plaything of childhood especially. The child loyal to its human nature—at whatever incomplete and dim stage of observation it may be—perceives in the ball the general expression of each object as well as of itself (the child) as a self-dependent whole and unity. It is above all important for the child, as a human being destined to become and in the future to *be* conscious, to perceive that which is inclosed in itself, in deed complete (*vollendeten)*, and so, as it were, the counterpart of himself and his opposite; for man seeks even as a child to develop himself as well as everything in Nature by means of that which is its opposite yet resembles it; and so the child likes to employ himself with the ball, even early in life, in order to cultivate and fashion himself, though unconsciously, through and by it, as that which is his opposite and yet resembles him. Indeed, the ball in the totality of its properties, as well be clearly shown in the course of our consideration, is in manifold respects as instructive a type for the child, as the All (the universe), with its phenomena, is for the adult.

There is yet another thing which gives to the ball not only a great charm for the children but likewise deep significance as a plaything, and so as a means of education; this is, that the child, feeling himself a whole, early seeks and must seek in conformity with his human nature and his destiny, even at the stage of unconsciousness, always to contemplate, to grasp, and to possess a whole, but never merely a part as such. He seeks to contemplate, to grasp, and to possess a whole in all things, and in each thing, or at least, by means of and with them. This can be abundantly proved in the history of the development of the individual human being as well as of whole nations, and of all humanity. Many phenomena in child-life, on the bright side of life as well as on the dark, can also be explained thereby. This whole for which the child seeks is also supplied to him by the ball.

Only we further notice in the life of the child how he—like the man in the fairy story—would like to *perceive* all *in* all, and also to make all from each. The ball is well adapted to fulfil this desire also of the child, being (as a whole inclosed in itself) the image of all in general, and also the particular image of individual things; as, for example, the apple, as well as all things which are spherical in form, and from which such manifoldness again develops, such as seed grains and the like. The ball—or, what is the same, the sphere—is actually the foundation, the germ, as it were, of all other forms which can therefore logically be developed from it in conformity with fixed simple laws; this fact will later be proved in the course of presenting the plays and the means of employment for children. Indeed, the sphere takes up immediately into itself all surrounding objects, since they are mirrored in it, as is justly said. Thus all which the child needs in the expressions of his life and activity, in the earliest beginning as well as in the later course of his development, are afforded by the ball; for, as it is a whole in itself, it is, as it were, the representative, the general expression of each whole. The child can see each whole and himself in it, as he makes each whole or each object from it, can repeatedly impress upon it his own image and thus stand face to face with himself.

In fostering the development of the child special attention must be given to these expressions of his life and activity, as these expressions are the foundation and means of the recognition of individual oneness, of unity as such, and of the accord of all things to which man is destined. Attention should also be given to that which clearly follows from the preceding, and which on account of its great importance must be brought forward here at the beginning of a play—namely, that the spirit in which a play is conceived and originated, as well as the spirit in which the plaything is treated and the play played, give to the play its significance and its worth, its efficient value to humanity. So also if the spirit by which Nature is created is comprehended by man, and if Nature is observed and treated in accordance with that comprehension, this spirit gives to Nature the significance which it has for man—a significance as true as it is deep and full of life, producing life as well as fostering and unfolding life.

But now how is the ball to be considered and used, especially for the first strengthening of the child as a whole, for the first exercise of his bodily powers, the development of the activity of his limbs and senses, as well as for the arousing and nourishing of his attention and of his free independent action?

This is wholly in accordance with the needs of the child and the nature of the ball.

We see how the little child likes so much to seize and grasp everything, even its own thumb or its other hand or fist if it has nothing else. We also see—which is certainly worthy of earnest consideration—how each hand by itself is well adapted to inclose a ball, as are also both hands together.

Therefore a ball is early given into the child's little hand, though at first only for grasping, for him to lay his little fingers round like rings, in order to comprehend its roundness and thus come to possess and hold it fast.

Even this clasping will soon strengthen the muscles of the child's fingers, hand, and arm, and also develop hand and fingers so as to fit them first of all for voluntary handling of the ball, and later for the right handling of other things. Everyone knows how much in the life of man, and even in the life of the child, depends on the proper grasping and the right handling of each thing in the actual as well as in the figurative sense. It is therefore inexpressibly important for the whole future life of the child that he should early learn to actually handle even one extraneous object on all sides.

This now requires that, as the child's use of limbs and senses increases, the ball may show itself to the child more as a thing separate from him; for at first the ball seems to be, as it were, one with the hand of the child himself, and seems to grow together with it like his fist; and this is well, as thus all future recognition of the child's surroundings and of the outer world come to the child by means of the ball.

As soon as the child is sufficiently developed to perceive the ball as a thing separate from himself, it will be easy for you, dear mother, and you, dear nurse, having previously fastened a string to the ball which you give into the child's little hand, to draw the ball gently by the string as if you wished to lift it out of the child's little hand. The child will hold the ball fast, the arm will rise as you lift the ball, and as you loosen the string the hand and arm will sink back from their own weight and through holding the ball fast; the feeling of the utterance of force, as well as the alternation of the movement, will soon delight the child; and the use of the arm in this activity gives dexterity to the arm and strengthens the arm and hand.

Now, dear mother, here is the beginning of your play and playing with your dear child through the mediation of the ball. From this, however, soon springs a quite new play, and thus also something new to the child, when, through a suitable drawing and lifting by the string, the ball escapes from the child's hand, and then quietly moves freely before him as individual object. Through this play is developed in the child the new feeling, the new perception of the object as a something now clasped, grasped, and handled, and now a freely active, opposite something.

One may say with deep conviction that even this simple activity is inexpressibly important for the child, for which reason it is to be repeated as a play with the child as often as possible. What the little one has up to this time directly felt so often by the touch of the mother's breast—union and separation—it now perceives outwardly in an object which can be grasped and clasped, and which has actually has been grasped and clasped. Thus the repetition of this play confirms, strengthens, and clears up in the mind of the child a feeling and perception deeply grounded in and important to the whole life of man—the feeling and perception of oneness and individuality, and of disjunction and separateness; also of present and past possession.

It is exceedingly important for the child which is to be developed, as well as for the adults who are to develop him (therefore, first of all, for the father and mother), that they (the adults) should not only perceive but should also suitably foster the awakening individual power and individual activity, and the awakening spirit of their child in the traces and slightest expressions found in the almost imperceptible beginning, so that the development of these qualities and this spirit may not be carried on by accidental, arbitrary, and disconnected exercises. It is also important to observe the progressive development of the strength as well as of the activity by means of a measuring object, for which also the play with the ball is in manifold ways the most suitable means for parents and child.

The idea of return or recurrence soon develops to the child's perception from the presence and absence; that of reunion, from the singlenesss and separateness; that of future repossession, from present and past possession; and so the ideas of being, having, and becoming are most important to the whole life of man in their results, and are therefore the dim perceptions which first dawn on the child.

From these perceptions there at once develop in the child's mind the three great perceptions of object, space, and time, which were at first one active perception. From the perceptions of being, having, and becoming in respect to space and object, and in connection with them, there soon develop also the new perceptions of present, past, and future in respect to time. Indeed, these ninefold perceptions which open to the child the portals of a new objective life, unfold themselves most clearly to the child by means of his constant play with the one single ball.

As we now find that all the development of the child has its foundation in almost imperceptible attainments and perceptions, and as we see that its first evanescent perceptions (almost imperceptible in the beginning) are fixed, increased, and clarified by innumerable repetitions—that is, by change—so we also remark that when two different and separate perceptions have been once received by the child, the third and the following perceptions necessarily proceed from them.

It is highly important for the careful and faithful fostering of the child that the fosterer should devote her whole attention to this truth early in the life of the child. It is also important early to observe, to retain, and therefore to connect with the objective, the linking together of the apparent and of the existent life, though this linking together is at first but dimly perceptible. For the future sure attainment of the earthly destiny of man not only depends on the comprehension of the nature of being, having, and becoming, of object, space, and time, as well as on the correct comprehension and consideration of present, past, and future, but man himself will, even in early childhood, in his triune nature and in conformity with the qualities combined in him in a manner corresponding to his nature, claim the attainment of this destiny. The more clearly you perceive this, parents and fosterers of childhood, and the more definitely you employ it in your fostering, the richer in results will be your education of children.

True, the natural and unspoiled feeling of the mother often hits upon the right thing to do; but this right thing is done by her too unconsciously and too unconnectedly, it is not repeated continuously enough; still less is it constantly and progressively developed, and so it is not logically enough built up. The mothers themselves, and yet more the nurses who undertake the mothers' business at a later time, only too easily abandon the path correctly pointed out by the pure motherly feeling, as could be easily demonstrated in many places; but we wish our endeavor to have that which the natural motherly feeling correctly though unconsciously suggests clearly recognized and constantly and progressively fostered, and so that life may become by this, for parents and child, a whole, the parts of which constantly, progressively, and reciprocally train one another—a whole which is consciously and progressively formed.

Thus the mother, guided by human feelings, connects the mute action, the becoming and become, with that which is perceptible only to the sight and touch—as, for instance, the action is connected with a definite place and object, and then, almost without exception, is connected with the audible word, the sign vanishing again almost as soon as it arises.

From the connection of opposites and the duality of the silent and the sounding, of the abiding and the vanishing, of the visible and the invisible, of the corporeal and the spiritual object, there goes forth to the child (who also bear this duality within himself in its unity) the objects as recognized by the mind, and thus held fast and the consciousness of the object; in this way consciousness itself develops in the child.

But consciousness itself belongs to the nature of man and is one with it. To become conscious of itself is the first task in the life of the child, as it is the task of the whole life of man. That this task may be accomplished, the child is even from his first appearance on earth surrounded by a definite place, and by objects: by the air blowing around all living creatures, as well as by the arousing, human, spiritual language of words; and so the animating word, at least the animating song, belong to each voluntary employment, and hence to playing with the child. Genuine, childlike human beings, mothers especially, as we have before seen, know this very well of themselves, therefore they undertake nothing with the child which they do not accompany with words spiritually exhaled and inhaled, even if obliged to confess that there can be no understanding of the spoken words by the child, as the general sense of hearing is not yet developed, still less the special hearing of words. So we find the mother, soon after the child's birth, caressing and talking to the little one; for that which can develop and originate, and is intended to do so, begins and must begin when as yet nothing exists but the conditions; the possibility, and, especially with human fostering, the dim anticipation of it. Thus is it with the attainment of man to consciousness, and the speech required and conditioned by that attainment to consciousness.

But now, how shall this word accompanying the play with the child, the play-speech of the child, be formed?

As childlike, as motherly, as playfully as possible; so motherly, that the mother creates it herself in the instant of using it with the child; that, quite inconsciously to herself, she creates it afresh in her own mind and from life so that it passes away as the word dies away; for this speech is to express the highest personal and most directly felt motherly life with the child; it is therefore impossible to put it down in black and white and represent it in its individuality, in its life-awakening and life-ravishing fullness, which is caused by momentary emotions of the mind and mind-union, by gaze, movement, and tone, as well as by song, etc.

Yet, in order as much as possible to come to an understanding with the dear fosterers of childhood, a hint at least, may be permitted to us.

Just as soon as the child's first capacity for speech is somewhat developed, we note how it follows out the sound in and by means of the movement which it remarks, and that it tries to imitate that sound with its own organs. "Tic, tac," we hear it say, in imitation of the movement of the pendulum and the striking of the clock. We hear it say, or sing, "Bim, bom," when the sound of the movement is more audible, or is comprehended as a sound. In the words *in* and *out* (*Innen und Aussen*), it is worthy of note that the child uses the vowel scale è—ah—oo, which symbolizes the movement from within.

Thoughtful and observant nurses can therefore observe many and beautiful things in all the first expressions of the workings of the child's inner life, especially when he begins actually to speak. These many and beautiful things which can be observed are an essential guidance in fostering the development of child. So we must perceive that the child, in the beginning of its use of speech, comprehends, designates, and retains through the words "tic, tac" rather the physical part of the movement; but by "bim, bom," he comprehends the movement more from the feeling, if one might so say, in the mind. And (if I may be permitted to express myself thus) through the "there, here," which comes later, the child follows the movement more as a thing of comparison, of recognition, and, in his dawning thought, more intellectually.

A further treatment of this subject must come later; now, we can only remark that it is highly important for the nurse to observe even the first and slightest traces of the articulate connection of the corporeal, intellectual, and spiritual nature of the child, and to observe it in its development from existence to sensation and thought, so that none of these directions of the child's nature should be arrested, or cultivated, in the development of the child at the expense of the others; but neither should any be repressed and neglected for the sake of the others. It appears important to us here, and we believe that all who quietly consider the first development of the child have already remarked, or will yet remark, that children, even from the first stage of development at the point to which they have arrived, are apt to indicate the swinging movement, "bim, bom," in a singing tone which approaches to song, and serves as such the emotional nature and its cultivation. They thus early and definitely point out that the center, the real foundation, the starting point of human development, and thus of the child's development, is the heart and emotions; but the training to action and to thought, the corporeal and spiritual, goes on constantly and inseparably by the side of it; and thought must form itself into action, and action resolve and clear itself in thought; but both have their roots in the emotional nature.

After these remarks, which are necessary for the knowledge, fostering, and protection of the primitive course of development, and of the laws of development of the human being, let us return to our childish play, but now with a presentiment of its deep significance.

By a slow and constant pull, the ball, hanging to a string, escapes from the child's hand, and "Bim, bom; bim, bom; tic, tac; tic, tac; here, there; here, there" sounds immediately from the mother's mouth, and indicates the movements of the ball.

This quite simple play admits of many changes by connecting it with different tones and words.

"See, child, see the ball—there, here; there, here."

The ball resting, "Here hangs the ball."

Slowly raising and lowering the ball by the string, "Up, down."

Letting it swing over an object (for example, the other hand placed crosswise): "There, here; there, here; over there, over here." Or, considerably lengthening the string, that the ball may swing slowly now toward the chid, now away from him, "Near, far; near, far"; or, "Now comes the ball; off goes the ball," or "The ball comes; the ball goes away"; or as a general indication, "Here it comes, there it goes."

Swinging the ball slowly in a circle: "Around, around; round to the right, round to the right; round to the left, round to the left."

Or, playing with the ball on a firm surface on the table before the child," Tap, tap, tap," letting the ball fall on different parts of the surface, especially in a vertical direction.

"Jump, ball, jump!" "See, now the ball jump! Jump! jump! jump!" letting the ball, held by the string, fall quickly and rebound by its own elasticity.

Or, helping it by a quick, short drawing of the string, "The ball jumps high"; "The ball can jump no more; it is tired; it lies down to sleep."

Quickly lifting the ball from the surface of the table on something, for example, the ball's box, "Hop up high"; or, raising it quickly over the box, "Hop over."

Twirling the ball on a surface in a horizontal position by the string, and then around a center, and imitating with the voice the more outward movement "r r r r" or merely

"Around, around."

And now raising the ball quickly by the string in a vertical direction into the air, and now hanging it, letting it twirl quietly and quickly backward, and now imitating more its inner movement by "l l l l" or "Turn thee, turn thee; swiftly, swiftly," or, pointing out the increasing speed of the movement, "Faster and faster."

The rolling on the surface can now be repeated, "Now to the right, now to the left"; and also can the turning of the ball hanging by the string be changed, "Now to the left, now to the right."

Then drawing the ball on a surface, "Pull, pull, pull." The string may at this point be laid in the child's hand, and string and hand grasped by the mother's hand and the ball drawn off the support: "Ah, there falls the ball!" This, which appears to the child an effect of his own action, delights him exceedingly.

Now the swinging movement may be again made with the ball in the air, either out from the middle, "Always wider," or from the outside toward the center "Always narrower."

As the child before perceived the circling movement, so it sees here the spiral widening and narrowing. So the movement of the ball can also be made in an oval line, "Lengthen out," or "Widen out."

In the same way, winding the ball on a string up and down round a stick in the form of a screw, "Always higher, always lower."

Or, merely drawing the ball on a string slowly up and letting it down, "High, low; high, low."

Now, the ball free from the string is allowed to roll on the surface. "Roll, roll, roll; there the ball runs!"

Or the ball can be made to recoil from a surface—for example, the ball-box or a book: "Come, ball, come again to baby"; "Here comes the ball"; "Catch the ball"; "The ball has fallen"; "Go for the ball"; "Look for the ball." The mother may lift the child to the place where the ball lies, in order that the little one may itself pick it up. If the child has attained to any degree of intellectual and physical development and strength. He must be allowed to pick up the ball himself when he throws it to the ground; and if the child is as yet too small and helpless to move himself for that purpose, he must be lifted to the place where the ball lies, especially if he himself has thrown the ball away; so that he may early experience the consequences and requirements of his own action, and discover that he must himself fulfil the requirements and bear the consequences. Effort should be early made not only to have the child make many and definite discoveries, but to have it retain them, as well in respect to their connections with each other as in respect to their results.

"Where is the ball?" "There is the ball again." "Ball, stay now with the baby."

Or, closing the hand over the ball, "Where is the ball?" Opening the hand again, "There is the ball."

A beautiful exercise, which is particularly pleasing to the child, is this: to make the ball turn constantly around its own center in the hollowed hand by a constant alteration of its center of gravity, or rather its point of support. This play can be well performed by moving the ball in a saucer in the same manner, by which the ball can be made to run around almost on the rim without falling. This representation can be accompanied by—"Dance prettily," or "See, the ball dances!" etc.

Or, raising the ball again by the string behind the other hand, placed crosswise, "Off!" etc. "Where!" etc. Bringing it again before the hand, "There!" etc.

Each of these exercises can now be repeated by itself as often as it gives the child pleasure. Through this repetition these exercises become just as important for the extension of the horizon of experience as for the greater clearness, definiteness, and distinctness of the child's experiences.

Thoughtful and attentive mothers and nurses can, however, perceive that all this proceeds from the play and the exercises themselves.

Then, lowering the ball into the some inclosed space—for

example, into the ball box—"Deep in!"

Shutting the ball up in the box again: "The ball is gone!" "It wants to sleep!" "My child is tired; yes, it is tired; it wants to sleep too!"

These and many other observation exercises offer in their connections innumerable changes for the employment of the child and for the awakening and nourishing of his intellectual as well as of his bodily activity; especially when the limbs of the child are so strengthened and developed in power that the ball can be given up to him, at least partly, and he can, by his capacity for speech, which is equally developing, already enter into a kind of conversation with his nurse; and yet we have here in the employment with the ball a whole side of childish employment and play to consider, namely, *the fact that the child likes so much to see all in each object, and to make all from each.* Many kinds of objects, inanimate and animate, can not fail to appear in the neighborhood of the child, in his surroundings; to the latter especially his attention is called involuntarily by their coming and going, or, intentionally, by his nurse. Life generally attracts life, as it awakens life. The child sees the coming of the dog and cat; in one case of the poodle or Spitz, in the other of the cat or kitten. The child notices the bird, the birdie in the cage, the sparrow at the window; the dove, the cock, and hen, the hen and chicken in the yard; he sees the carriage, and the horse, etc.

In conformity with this quality and requirement of the child, the swinging ball can now become a birdie: "See how the birdie flies, now here, now there!"

Now the springing ball can become a kitten "There springs the kitty on the bench."

Now a dog: "Hop goes the dog over the hedge."

Now the ball becomes a chicken: "Tip, tap, tap, the chicken comes running."

Now the cock: "Tap, tap, tap, the cock picks up the corn."

Now a squirrel which climbs up the tree, going round and round it, or in the same manner climbs down.

Now a miner: "He goes deep down into the shaft."

Or the ball without a string: now the sheep which we must watch; now the horse or colt which springs away; now the dog which comes running, "Bow, wow, wow!" But now, again the ball on the string, on the carriage (or, if it is winter, on the sled or sleigh) which is drawn; and a hundred other things.

The thought now impresses itself upon us as an important one, that by one and the same object, and that, moreover, an inanimate object (in this case the ball), are perceived, and as it were made, many kinds of objects, and above all lives ones; from which follows another thought that objects are brought before the child by words here (as also indeed in life) which it has not yet even once seen; which are not to be found at all in its neighborhood.

Yet this might appear inadmissible to many a one who has not yet deeply and universally enough entered into the course of development of the child's life and its conditions, although we have already pointed out its existence in the nature and life of the child. We will therefore briefly justify this procedure, without, however, penetrating deeply into human nature, in which it could be very easily demonstrated as necessary and as required; but this is not the place for it. At some time the anticipation and thus the inner recognition of the special and the general, will be unfolded to the child. But this takes place when, as already remarked, the opposites, having yet some similarity, are compared with one another. Then also the fewer special similarities and qualities that the means of perception or the object used to play with has with the presented object (which, of course, must be connected by preceding connecting links), the more skilled the child becomes thereby; he now considers the actual object in order to obtain a clear impression of it and of its special qualities, so as to rise from the perception of the object to that of its kind, and from the perception of the kind to that of its species, etc.

The second remark is, that objects are here brought before the child which indeed the playing adult has seen, but which as yet the playing child has not seen at all. Though this is not to be scrupulously avoided, as little is it to be thoughtlessly carried too far; kept within right limits it justifies itself to any simple and straight forward mind. The life and the course of development of the human being and the laws of this development make this repeat itself with the most developed man, for, as man is a being destined to attain increasing consciousness, so he is also to become and be a reasoning and judging being. Besides, man has a peculiar presaging power of imagination, as indeed also—what must never be forgotten, but always kept in view as important and guiding—the newborn child is not merely to become a man, *but the man already appears and indeed is in the child with all his talents and the unity of his nature.*

Objects not yet seen in life by the child may therefore be introduced to him through word and playthings that represent these objects, but with the following restriction: this introduction (as, for example, in the preceding pages, of the squirrel) ought not to take place before the child—who is through frequent repetition quite familiar with the object, near, already often seen, and always possible to be seen again (for example, the kitten)—in the qualities of the personifying object (here of the ball), has recognized the qualities of the personified object (here of the kitten), and likewise has seen in and through the first (the ball) the second (the kitten); has learned to represent it, for example, by the jumping. Now the child has also noticed the climbing of the cat and when it is said, as above, "The squirrel climbs," etc., the child quickly comes to the conclusion that the squirrel is a living thing that climbs. This is enough to excite its attention, so that when he some day sees a squirrel, and the squirrel is named to him as such, he fixes his eye upon it sharply, and perhaps, indeed, even without hearing its name, recognizes it as such from this quality and other connections. This is a sufficient hint for the justification of this childlike, motherly, and (in the nursery) domestic procedure.

We now go back to the contemplation of the ball as the first plaything, and bring into prominence as essential the fact that it (being, as it were, the representative and means of perception of all that is contained in and rests in itself) offers to be perceived, produced, and handled only the fundamental form, as it were the rough sketch of all which can present itself as a whole and can act spontaneously as such; so that several of the phenomena of the ball—such as presence, departure, return, seeking, finding, getting, catching, grasping, holding, rolling, sliding, turning, etc.—can be represented by each of the said objects as well as by the ball, which is, just on that account, such as excellent and attractive plaything for the child. But though, as just stated, several of the phenomena of the ball can be represented by each of the said objects, this is not the case with all the phenomena—for instance, the multifariousness of movement. For this reason, in order to increase the powers and advance the development of the child, the plays carried through with the ball are, as the opportunity or the demand is made, given in part with other objects—for example, an apple, a handkerchief, a ball of thread, a key, a nut, a flower, etc.—and these objects are thus brought before the child in various kinds of activity. But the ball always remains as the uniting and explaining object, and thus the true means of connection and understanding, and the very plaything to connect the child with his nurses and his surroundings.

If the child is now old enough to sit alone and likes to do so, and also to creep or drag himself from one place to another, the play with the ball can be essentially and efficiently extended. Thus a quilt is spread in the room, the child seated on it and a ball, now with, now without a string, given to him for his own spontaneous handling. Also, if it can be easily accomplished, a ball of suitable size can be fastened by a sufficiently strong cord to the ceiling of the room, so that the child can at times employ himself with swinging himself with the ball, and it times can raise himself up, and so can stand by means of it. He will thus learn to hold himself more surely in equilibrium, and to stand more easily than if he raises himself up by a body which stands firmly—a chair, or a bench—which does away with the necessity for him to maintain his own center of gravity; and if he falls, the falls is less painful, with a good quilt to fall on. Yet more suitable is it, in reference to the child's learning to stand, that the ball, proportionately increased in size and fastened to a strong and sufficiently long string, be given into the hand of the child seated on a sufficiently thick quilt, with the directions to hold it firmly. Now the attempt is made to raise the child higher and higher by means of the cord which is fastened to the ball. The raising and lowering will please the child, as well as strengthen the muscles of the whole body, hips and thigh especially. If he is thus raised by means of the ball and string to a standing position, he can soon easily stand independently.

Here is now the point, as beautiful as it is important, where the life and activity of further also, at times when his business permits, can exert a fostering and developing influence on the life of the child; and the ball here again appears as a connecting link between child and father, as it was at an earlier period between child and mother. The child in the father's company is to grow up, as it were, climb up to him, and by his aid is to steady itself, all this is now offered in manifold shapes by the above given play with the ball, by which, in order to render it again prominent, the father comes into his right relation to the child, calling out his strength, etc. (consideration, reflection), but also using and thus developing strength, etc. By means of the earlier play, especially of that connected with speech, the mother, with all her mildness, enters into the life of the child.

So the first play of the child with the ball is now revealed in its nature as well as in its application and its general effects. Through this is given to you, dear parents, for your child, what is as beneficial as it is important—the means for his constantly progressive development, from the first activity of the limbs and senses up to independent sitting and voluntary self-occupation, and a means is given of leading towards the constant fostering of these developments. We now see how comprehensively the child's life is satisfied by the play with the ball.

We see, in proportion as the first child's plays which we have given are apparently simple and transient, as they are born at the moment and are dropped again at the moment and supplanted by others; in proportion as the child is at first not capable of receiving them in their complex details, just in that proportion are they important for the unfolding and the growth of the child in all ways; for since we are thoroughly penetrated by the conviction that the movements of the young and delicate mind of the child, although as yet so small as to be almost unnoticeable, are of the most essential consequences to the whole future life of the child, therefore no perception is more important for the child and his future life and action than that of the unity of all manifoldness and that of the living correlation between both, and these two perceptions are shown to the child as definitely as manifoldly by the ball as appears from what follows.

It is evident to the child that all the various plays proceed from the single ball, and that in their phenomena refer again to the uniting ball; they make known the manifoldness resting in the ball, which is itself single; they proceed from unity and again lead back to unity. In the second and also opposite view, the play is considered from the child outward; all activity, although connected with the ball, proceeds definitely from the child (who is in himself a unit), and, although using the ball as a means, refers to the child, who is in himself a unit. The child is in himself unity and manifoldness, and destined to develop this unity and manifoldness by the surrounding outer world; and for this, also, the ball serves through the play with it, but especially by its individuality and its properties; for the ball itself, being the representative of all objects, is the unity and union of the essential properties of all objects. Thus the ball shows contents, mass, sphere, space, form, size, and figure; it bears within itself an independent power (elasticity), and hence it has rest and movement, and consequently stability and spontaneity; it offers even color, and at least calls forth sound; it is indeed heavy—that is, it is attracted—and thus shares in the general property if all bodies. Therefore the ball, by its fall, by its quicker movement on a shorter and its slower movement on a longer string, leads to the consideration of the most important phenomena and laws of earth-life and the life of Nature, of attraction in general, and first of all of the attraction of the earth, especially of its laws and limitations, in which and through which only, the child himself lives and has his being as a human dweller on the earth, since he lives and exists only through the breathing in of the air. Therefore the ball, as a connecting plaything between parent and child, places man in the midst of all, on his entrance into the world and with the activity of his limbs and senses, in the midst of all phenomena and perceptions of Nature, as of all limitations of Nature, and of all life; for what is more attractive than life? But to place man through a skillful education in the understanding of and in harmony with Nature and life, and to maintain him in it with consciousness and circumspection, can not be done too early.

Hence the ball, as we have already seen in many ways, is a bond of connection between mother and child, between parent and child—it is a connection between the child and his nearest surroundings—and thus is it in general a bond of connection between the child and Nature; and the ball connects the child with Nature as much as the universe connects man with God.

As now the ball, by its individuality and by means of the play with it, places man, even in childhood, in the midst of the life of Nature and of all life, and of all life, and makes itself perceived and felt in it, so in like manner it makes itself perceived and felt in it, so in like manner it makes the child early to feel and find himself in the midst of his own life, in the midst of his perceptive (feeling), his operative and creative, and his comparing (thinking) activity. The ball and the play with the ball lay hold of the whole man as a child, in respect to his body as well as in respect to his mind and soul. Thus, in order to bring forward with precision one phenomenon, only one, and here the nearest to us, which has been mentioned the ball (even in its first swinging movement, if the movement is several times and often repeated, and by the words "tic tac, tic tac," the child is made to notice the movement through space and its regular intervals and remember it) has an exciting effects on the body of the child, which effect is expressed by hopping, also a measured movement. But it is not even this single play, developed in harmony with the whole human being, important for his whole life? Is it not even the dim, how much more yet the developed, feeling of the correct time, that is, the feeling of tact or the right instant at which to exert an influence on another by his activity, which later often preserves man from so many disagreeable experiences? And does not this depend on the earlier development of man which always remembers what was opportune, and which is least retarded when it finds itself in harmony with the occasion.

The movement, on the contrary, predominantly full of life and expression, which is comprised in and represented by "bim, bom," etc., acts on the heart; this fact is made known in the course of the development of the child by his laughter as a expression of the arousing of emotions and of the use of his eyes. Do we not already see by this how beneficial, melodious, and therefore harmonious, training is for man at an early stage of his being? But the movement, more suggestive of comparison, comprehended in and represented by the words "there, here," acts predominantly on the intellect, and makes itself known in the course of the child's development by the imperfect speech connected with it as the spontaneous expression of the child's awakening power of thought; and do we not find indicated in this already the peculiarity and requirement of the human mind to render itself intelligible, to clarify itself by communication with others?

As now each of the single plays severally considered lay hold upon the child early in the trinity of his nature as creating, feeling, and thinking, so do yet more the playful employments considered as a whole. The attentive observer can easily perceive that one whole series of the plays belong pre-eminently to the actual, external, and creative life, or at least refer to it; these may be even described as useful in a certain point of view. With another series of plays, each, without reference to anything extraneous, suffices for itself, because an inner unity, a life which is in itself single, appears in an outward manifoldness which harmonizes with it. The representation of these plays, through which inner unity (existence) appears in and by means of harmonious variety, and shines forth from it, as it were, can not receive a more significant designation than beautiful. So in the third series of plays each single play is likewise only attractive to the child in, by and through its various relations, properties, and connections, each of which has been already suggested—indeed, indicated inwardly—before it appeared outwardly, and therefore before it was recognized. One can not but say of these plays that they early enchain the child's attention on account of their truth, though unconsciously to the little one himself, and perhaps unrecognized by him through this whole life.

Thus, without bringing out from the mentioned plays authentic proofs for the stated series, which is very possible to a thoughtful consideration, we here show only how directly the course of childish employments, to which the path is broken by the first child-plays (which, beginning from the ball, advancing constantly according to inner laws, is now to be pursued uninterruptedly in the production of means for the child's employment), early leads the child to a harmonious training for usefulness, beauty, and truth; and how means are early given to the parents to attain the harmonious cultivation of their child; we are to consider to which side of the cultivation he predominantly inclines; since one excludes the other no more than life, art, and science do, so man, and still more the child, ought not to be educated and cultivated one-sidedly and exclusively for the one or the other.

The cultivation of the mental power of the child in different directions is also attained by the use of the ball as the first plaything. The child learns by the use of it to keep an object in view not only in a state of rest, but also in the changes of its phenomena. The play carried on with the ball awaken and exercise the power of the child's intellect to place again before himself and object not present to his bodily eyes, to perceive it inwardly even when the outward appearance has vanished. These plays awaken and exercise the power of representing, of remembering, of retaining in remembrance an object seen formerly, of again thinking of it—that is , they foster the memory.

The awakening and fostering of the powers of the mind

to compare, to conclude, to judge, to think, have been already discussed, and every observer can easily see how by these plays the powers are further awakened and exercised in the child, how they continue to develop and are more and more formed within. Only, we must remark, what is capable of demonstration, that this most delicate growth of the mind is germinated and fostered quietly and gradually by means of the actions, feelings, and thoughts of the mother, and by means of her love, faith, and hope with respect to the child, although yet so imperceptibly in the child's life thus connected with the mother's—by means of the ball and the play with the ball.

We see the human being as a child, yes, even as an infant, placed in the midst of his life, as of all life, by means of the ball and the play with the ball; for his own life, his mother's life, his father's life, and the life of all his surroundings become to him thus inwardly vital and jointly objective, as the life and the love of the mother as become one and objective to him in the fullness of the mother's breast which afford him nourishment, which itself appears to him a ball, and in his all.

Again, dear mothers, dear fathers, and nurses, do not think and believe that the child, in his predominantly physical, indeed as yet quite helpless stage of development, is not susceptible to all that has been mentioned. You err deeply, you err to the great detriment of the whole future life of your child and the fruits of your otherwise strenuous care of the child. The child is just as susceptible to it as the kernel hidden deeply in the earth in darkness, or the bud on the tree covered by hard scales even resembling a stone, are sensitive to the return of the sun in spring or even to a warm but evanescent breath of air. He, then, who does not already perceive and foster consciously and circumspectly the traces of the future development of the future life of the child when still hidden in the depths and in the night, he also will not clearly perceive them, nor proportionately, or at least not sufficingly, foster them even when they lie open before him. Only through the comprehension of the connection, as fervent as it is full of life; or rather of the eternal trinity—of the invisible, the invisibly perceptible, and the visible—is life itself comprehended.

But one thing remains for us to bring forward in the consideration and contemplation of the plays with the ball: this is the definite, clear, and legitimate development of the child's capacity for speech in the progressive course of the play. As the child, as has been demonstrated in many ways, is placed by this playing in the midst of Nature and of life, or rather finds itself buoyant with life, so it is also by this playing placed in the midst of its capacity for speech, of the legitimate development of that capacity, or rather finds and quietly unfolds itself therein.

A few hints from the many which could be given and clearly presented on the subject must here and now suffice; this subject will be later taken up again and treated of by itself. Here on that subject we will give as hints only the following: The language which accompanies the first child-play seems to be clear, precise, full, significant, simple, and yet completely satisfying. Even the first words of it, to which the play gave rise and which the child discovered, and ever anew discovers, contain the whole material of words—that is, in these words are immediately given vowel sounds, open and closed sounds. Each appear clear and distinct, each comes forth pure in its nature in the childish words, bim, bom (boum). So in au (aou) are defined and given the three fundamental voice sounds, a, o, u, and in i their relating, middle, or conclusion; and thus through them is given the complete compass of vowel sounds in language. Also, the compass of language brought into the employment by the play, slight as it appear, embraces the whole province of language proceeding from the perception and comprehension of the object in space. The words used are mostly word stems or roots, and from them develops speech full of life, regular and all-sided, as an image of the two great worlds, the inner and the outer world.

The ball gives to the child all this, and many another thing, which is not at all retained by word as an outside phenomenon in its individualities, and joins itself to all as the first childish plaything; through it the little one develops himself; by it is strengthened in the unity of his nature and life, proportionally in body and in spirit. It is enough that in the first plays with the ball the life of the child makes itself known, and the outer world makes itself known to the child in unity.

5

Educating Developing Child

It has, in the course of these expositions, been repeatedly asserted—and indeed it was first asserted at the conclusion of the first of them—that the giving of a new play by no means precludes the further use of the preceding and earlier plays. But, on the contrary, the use of the preceding play for some time longer with the new play, and alternating with it, makes the application of the new play so much the easier and more widely significant. On the other hand, the practice of the new play following has a retroactive effect on the more animated and thoughtful, as well as on the more intelligent and freer use of the preceding plays in general. It was also stated that the plays are in themselves a whole, and, indeed, a whole the parts of which develop from one another, and their spirit is felt and recognized as a spirit of union and singleness of purpose. So also is the development of the child himself felt and perceived, and therefore striven for by himself as well as by his observant nurse, as a whole constantly unfolding from itself; hence it receives further nurture.

Yet these playthings, or rather the comprehension of the play and playing of the child as a great *living whole* dependent upon Nature and life in all relations, show also a different quality. They show, namely, that they continue to unfold in the progressive course of the development and education of the child in a logical sequence; and yet, as it were in harmony with the growth of the child, and unfold themselves a new and generate new things from themselves in their use, in their application, and in a manner suited to the course and the then existing stage of the child's development.

Let us now in this connection stops here at the first the simplest of the playthings, at the ball.

As the strength of the child develops, the use of the ball becomes more varied, certainly freer, and I might say more personal. So as, for example, the child in the beginning merely lets the ball roll from the box on the table and fall back into the box; then next he lets the ball run back from the cup into the box; from the box again into the cup, and lets it roll round in the cup (both of these acts are frequently repeated actual facts of the first child life and child play), so will the child also very soon—as soon as he has perceived that he can hollow his little hand like a cup—let the little ball run from one hand into the other (as the child, and especially the little girl, later employs itself for a long time merely by pouring water or sand from one vessel into another alternately). This activity of the child is now taken up and imitated. It is repeated, and at the same time extended by letting the ball run from one hand into the other, but also at the same time—in order to render prominent the resting in the different hands—inclosing and hiding it now in one hand, now in the other, but again showing it alternately at rest now on one hand, now on the other.

The child (like the man) would like to learn the *significance* of what happens around him. This is the foundation of Greek choruses, especially in tragedy. This, too, is the foundation of very many productions in the realm of legends and fairy tales, and is indeed the cause of many phenomena in actual history. This is the result of deeply rooted consciousness, the at first deeply slumbering premonition of being surrounded by that which is higher and more conscious than ourselves. In this unconscious premonition the child calls upon all which surrounds him, and particularly on the conscious, speaking beings about him, to tell him this *meaning*, or at least give him some information or hint concerning the kind of relation which exists between things. Indeed, the child demands even of the mute object that it tell him its meaning, and let him perceive these relations. This premonition and demand of the innermost child nature shows itself to all who have the care of children, and especially to the mother. By the satisfaction of this premonition and this demand the child will grow to love and reverence its parents, and acquire respectful recognition of age and experience. The nurse may, therefore, when she brings the child's own play to his more definite perception by imitating it, sing to him as follows:

> Over there,
> Over here;
> Now it is there;
> Now it is here;
> Now it is far,
> Now it is near;
> I see now no more
> What just now I saw.

Or :

> Go there, here; there, here; there, here;
> Like a shuttle, wander, dear.
> You have woven long enough
> For a yard-long piece of stuff.

It is scarcely necessary to say that through this play the interval of time quickly consumed in weaving is symbolized. It is likewise by no means necessary, still less perhaps is it required, that this should be expressed by the child, or even to him. The significance lies open to the feeling, to the emotion, to the perception of the child when the little one complainingly or entreatingly comes to his mother, saying, "Mother, the time seems long to me; what shall I do?" He is briefly answered, "Weave"— that is, in other words, "Busy yourself with the means around you." I believe nothing more is needed for thinking and sensible parents, mothers and nurses, in order to perceive thoroughly the inner constant coherence even of the first and smallest of the child plays with the later manlike professional or business life of the human being now still in the stage of childhood. Or the simple play can be accompanied by singing the words:

Over there,
Over here,
It quickly
Can spring;
And clearly
I sing
A song to it, dear.

In this is indicated the harmony, the accord of the inner, experiencing life with the outer, active life, and the animating, delightful influence of the play.

Yet, before we advance further in the onward development of the free play with the ball, we will first pause to consider another side of the play with the ball, which is in a certain respect related to it.

It will not have escaped the notice of the reader of this book that whenever an opportunity presents itself to children they throw the ball upon an *inclined* surface—for example, on a roof—that the ball may roll down it, and they standing below may catch it in the hand.

Seeing this, one can sing with the child, and according to his experience:

Off I send thee;
Yet thou lov'st me,
And show'st to me
Thy constancy.
The shortest track
Will bring thee back,
Straight back to me.

The appearance and meaning of this play are inclination and union; the straight path is under certain conditions the nearest way, at least the straight line is always the shortest. Or, further:

The higher goes my ball,
The swifter it will fall;
And yet I always see
It coming back to me.

Object observed and meaning: the greater the space through which it falls and the longer the unobstructed line of its fall, the quicker is the movement, the stronger is the action and power of the falling body. If one wishes to point out this latter phenomenon for children somewhat older, one can add, singing to the ball as if from the mouth of the child:

Yes, the greater space
Does not destroy your force,
But make it more, of course.
Did I not perceive it,
I scarcely would believe it.

Yet the child is delighted not only by the rebound of the ball from the slanting and the catching it again, but also with its rebound from the *flat wall*, as will be noticed everywhere where children are. One can sing to the child again, as it were, from its own mouth, the following. We will, however, let the little songs, for better understanding, follow in descending series:

I throw my ball against the wall,
Back to my hand now flies my ball.
Again I throw it far away,
But far from me it will not stay.
O ball ! what can the reason be,
Thou always comest back to me!

This is a hint of the elasticity of the ball, etc.

Or :

I long to catch thee,
Quickly to snatch thee;
Come like an arrow
Let loose from a bow;
Come like the wind
Which from hill-tops doth blow.
Thou bringest to me
Much pleasure, much glee.

Or :

Fly from the wall,
Back to me, ball !
And as you spring,
Joy to me bring !

Or, briefly :

Hand,
Wall;
Spring,
Ball.

Now, since the child has practiced itself in this way in catching the ball, we return to the free manipulation of it, or rather to the manipulation of it in perfectly free space. We were considering above the play in which the child threw the ball from one hand to the other; now we will also bring into the play the act of throwing it or tossing it vertically into the air. The child first tosses the ball into the air, then catches it again with the same hand, tosses it into the other hand from this again back into the first hand, which, as in the beginning of the play, tosses it again into the air, and again catches it, then again tosses it into the other hand, and so goes on as before. Upon this one can sing to the child, and perhaps later sing *with* him:

Go up,
Down fall;
Fly off,
Come, ball.

Up to this point we have merely represented plays in which the child played alone. But the pleasure and liveliness, and, as the children themselves call it, the *fun* of the play, will soon bring a second, a companion to the one player.

They can then again begin with the simple tossing back and forth to each other, and they can themselves sing, or the nurse can at first sing to them or with them, as above indicated:

Over there,
Over here,
Quickly
'Twill spring;
Clearly
We'll sing.
A song to it, dear;
A song to it, dear.

But this play can also soon, especially for skillful children, receive a very simple but considerably extended alteration. Instead of the tossing being done from the right hand into the left hand opposite, or from both hands into both hands as in the former play, it can now be varied by oblique movements, for example, thus: from the *right* hand of the first the ball goes in an oblique direction to the *right* hand of the second boy; from *this* hand again in a straight direction to the *left* hand of the first, and from *this* again in a slanting direction to the *left* hand of the second boy; *he* now with his *left* hand throws the ball back into the *right* hand of the first boy, who then begin the play anew. To this can be sung:

> There and here,
> Straight across,
> And then oblique.
> There and here,
> Straight across,
> And then oblique.
> We will tightly
> Weave in playing.
> Good work wins the
> Mother's praises;
> But, alas ! now
> All is in pieces

A symbolical portrayal of an activity without any visible results.

But the first play, the simple throwing or tossing to one another, may also be extended in the following beautiful manner: While the two players toss the ball to each other, they either alternately or both at the same time recede from each other by a short step, and at the same time, in proportion to the increasing distance, toss the ball to one another in a higher and higher arch, and sing:

> Going high, now,
> Lightly fly now,
> In an arc.

Always farther,
Always farther
  Be the mark.

A very beautiful alteration in the form of an extension to this play may be produced if *two* balls are taken, so that each player holds one which he tosses to his fellow; this play can be accompanied by the following word, sung or spoken:

If now we balls are *two*,
We'll show you something new;
See ! now a race we try,
And in a race we fly,
Each to the other's hand.

But this play can be also sung alone by a child practiced in these exercises, in which case the conclusion of the song is different, viz.:

Each to the other hand.

It can be seen from this how these plays are not only precisely adapted to the developed strength and acquired skill of the child, but that also both strength and skill are developed by the plays, which are a measure of their development.

But more than two, three, or four children, placing themselves in a triangle or quadrangle, can at the same time takes part in this play, so that the first child always throws the ball to the second child, the second to the third, and so on. Since now a greater interval of time elapses before the ball comes to be caught, the desire is increased in the child that the ball may now also come to him; this the children can now again sing, for example:

Ball, I have
A great desire
  You to seize;
Quickly come here,
  If you please.

If there are *four*, *five*, or *six* children or more, one can sing to them, and they can sing to themselves, or rather to their ball:

Gayly to wander
From one to another,
Ball, fly up so,
High in a bow.
For you to seize
Will me much please.

The expression of both is the yearning to subordinate one's self to a higher general law of life, and to a higher requirement of life.

When the number of the playing children increases to six, or perhaps eight, and the ability to play has risen to skillfulness—indeed, to a high degree of accomplishment—one can also bring into the play two or more balls in the proportion to the number of children; for example, a *green*, a *red*, a *yellow*, so that they, like flowers, may wind themselves into a garland. To this may be sung:

Dear little balls,
  Your places take,
Swinging and dancing,
  A wreath to make,
You, like flowers
  Intertwining,
Should be ready
  For combining.

Here enters now especially the subordination to the law of motion, which is just what makes the orderly, concerted, and especially the circling movements and activities of all plays, not only so animating, but also so formative, so uniting. Being in harmony not only with the higher life of Nature, but even with the higher human life, and introducing the child into those phases of life these plays unfold to receive and become penetrated by these two kinds of life, and they can not be too carefully cultivated, and can not be represented with too much purity, clearness, and accordance with the laws of life.

We now again return to the plays in which an outside foreign object (for example, a wall) is brought into the play.

These plays admit of new adaptations, in which two or more children take part, especially now since the development of the whole system of plays has made some essential progress. The familiar game of the *apprentice* and *master workman* finds here not only a place quite suitable for it, but it comes forth here wholly rejuvenated from the living whole of the plays, and as a new thing. We will assume that there are four children of about the same age and development. The first, A (for example, Augustus), begins to throw the ball at the wall, so that it rebounds and falls into his hand, held open to catch it; he sings, meanwhile, and the rest accompany him in chorus:

> Tap, tap, tap !
> Springing from the wall straight back,
> You to catch will well please me;
> An apprentice then I'll be.

One after another of the four players takes his turn in throwing the ball; those who could not catch the ball but let it fall to the ground remain mere candidates, and must begin anew with the next round of the game. We will suppose this to have been the case with B (for example, Bernhard).

Now the second round begins, or, in other words, the new contest. The first player, A, sings; the others accompany him, singing, or merely saying, in chorus:

> Tap, tap, tap !
> Quickly from the wall spring back;
> You to catch will well please me;
> One time, two times, three times, four times, five times,
> Then a journeyman I'll be.

We will assume A to have also here again fortunately succeeded and attained the rank of journeyman. But B, who in the first round did not reach the rank of apprentice, but was obliged to remain in the rank of candidacy, must now begin anew, as above said, and we will assume that he now attains the rank of apprentice.

Now steps forward C (for example, Carl). He succeeds likewise as did A; for he arose to the rank of an apprentice in the first game, and we assume that he, like A, now ascends to the rank of journeyman. D, however, can not fulfil the requirements for admission to this rank; he can not catch the ball once during the singing of the journeyman song; but the ball sinks to the ground before the song is ended, and hence D must remain in the rank of apprentice. A and C alone have reached the journeyman stage.

Now begin the *third* round. A again steps forth first. The others accompany him, singing, or merely speaking, in chorus:

> Tap, tap, tap !
> Springing from the wall far back,
> You to catch will well please me;
> One time, two times, three times, ... ten times,
> Then I can a master be.

And A has now actually become a *master*. B must repeat the song of the *journeyman* stage and fulfil its requirements, which D must also afterward do. C also raises himself to the rank of *master*. Thus A and C are now *masters*, B and D *journeymen*.

Now begins the *fourth* round.

A again first enters the lists; he says or sings, and the other accompany him in chorus:

> Tap, tap, tap !
> Springing from the wall high up,
> You to catch will well please me;
> One time, two times, three times, ... twenty times,
> A head master then I'll be.

But A has not fulfilled the requirement of the song; he yet remains at the *master* stage.

B sings the master song and rises to a *master*.

C attains the *head-master* stage. D only can not fulfil the demands of the master stage, but remains at the *journeyman* stage.

What an *image* of life is now given to the child in this simple play, carried out only in its pettiest connections ! *What genuine education* for life, and what and education for *genuine life !* What a comprehensive *instruction* about life—about true life—taking the whole human being into consideration ! What an *exercise* for life as it as, and is to be! Are there yet directions needed as to the details? Not only the developed but the harmoniously developed strength, not only the dominion over the outward but the unison and harmony of the outward with the inward, leads to the beautiful goal of life.

But that the plays may lead to this, it is by no means sufficient to resign the plays to the children; but it is above all quite essential that the spirit of these plays, as in general the genuine spirit of all plays and of each play, should live in the observant mother or nurse, and, above all, in the first genuine teacher. For only on condition that in him lives the genuine spirit of play—i.e., the true spirit of life—will he call it forth in the children. Through this even the very neighborhood of such a teacher has an educating effect—that is to say, it acts like a magnet, drawing forth the nobleness, elevation, pure humanity lying in the disposition of the child. Therefore now all our thoughts and efforts, all our meditations and aspirations, should be directed to educating and training mothers and nurses for such fostering of childhood and humanity. I shall be obliged to return to this subject at the close of this article. I must now, first of all, complete the discussion of the play lying before us.

That not only the strength called into activity leads to the constant development of the whole life, but that the strength adjusted in every direction to the requirements of life, so as to produce a harmony, has the same result, can be taught to the child by the simple play in which the ball is thrown down to a level plane surface, and bounding from his perpendicularly into the air, is driven back again and again by the flat hand to the plane surface. This play can be accompanied by the words sung or spoken by the child, or by the attentive teacher:

Spring ! spring ! spring !
You are a brave thing;
On the ground you will not lie,
Always up from it you fly.
    Your own force
    Does, of course,
  Take you up so high.

The child not only finds outside of himself in play, indeed by his play, and indeed by his plaything the ball (although it be a so-called lifeless body), that use of the strength increases the strength, and that orderly employment of the strength prolongs its use; but he perceives this fact of his own accord, and as a fact of his own nature, and not merely as an external fact limited in its application to his play or to his plaything. Therefore the child now likes to sing at each suitable opportunity to its ball, playing with it at the same time:

How much my ball I prize !
My strength I exercise—
All my strength on thee.
Joy thou bringest me.

To catch thee I must try
Quickly to spring, and high.
If I can succeed,
I am glad, Indeed.

When to catch I'm ready,
Must my eye be steady,
And, in glad play, see
No other aim than thee.

My hollowed hands I learn
Always to thee to turn;
If you thou dost in them fall,
How glad I am, my ball !

How much my ball I prize !
My strength I exercise—
All my strength on thee.
Dear ball, stay with me !

Hence the meaning of the play is to apply a similar procedure to a solution of the highest problem of life, and *to hold fast the one high purpose amid all the vicissitudes of time and place.*

Little as it has been possible for us up to this point to present and exhaustive or complete view of the manifold details of the plays and occupations already discussed and tested in many of their applications, and to show them in their influence upon the whole human being, in their developing and training effects on the human being as a child, yet we hope that we have proved our thesis even through this brief presentation from life, since it is derived clearly and unequivocally as a strict consequence from our insight into child nature. We have tried to show that through such a childhood and child nurture as that here aimed at and mapped out, the child is influenced, developed, and cultivated, in the totality of his nature and in the all-sidedness of his being and life. You will also perceive how, through this, it will be quite sufficient for the purpose of the education of children (and this the only true purpose) that there may be offered to the child through these plays and occupations—that is, through the free sway and action of their pure and uniting influence (especially in the earliest and first foundations of this education), and in such a form that he may receive it into his life—all that we always yearn to obtain for him as his portion on his long life-path.

It is therefore impossible for us longer to repress the thought and wish that these plays might be an undisputed possession of the child-world. And then with this the genuine and original spirit of child life, and of humanity, could make itself everywhere free, and through the spirit of these plays be clearly recognized.

But now how shall we reach this result most effectively and easily, and at the same time make sure that these plays shall be also the possession of the individual families, and that their spirit, above all, may be the spirit of the individual family life, of the family sitting-room as well as of the nursery? Even through the introduction of these plays and occupations into the numerous infant schools already existing in many places, where the children till now were too little employed, or not judiciously— that is to say, not self-actively enough. Something essential could be gained by their introduction into these infant schools, because the children would then bring these fundamental and culture-giving occupations home with them from the school and introduce them into the family life. These would serve for judicious and useful self-occupation and further culture for themselves, as well as for their brothers and sisters, and for their companions and playmates; and these things would even be worthy of the notice of their parents. However, we must consider these plays in their reference to the totality of human development, and on account of their pure human influence, as *a common possession of the whole child-world*. The mere introduction into the institutions for the care of little children, and the so-called infant schools now existing, greatly as its realization is to be desired and striven for, can therefore, in many respect, especially for the reasons just given, by no means suffice. But these plays should first of all become a common possession of those families whose children (so greatly needing satisfactory care and nurture) are not provided for by such institutions. Therefore, in such places as are pointed out by the demands of life as well as by the favourableness of the situation, there should be *established by the union* of intelligent families blessed with children of the proper age, such institutions for the bodily as well as spiritual nurture of the whole period of infancy, in which under the guidance of one trained for the purpose, the activity of the children should be carefully fostered and nourished in the way here pointed out, although at first only during a few hours of the day.

The children will thus be soon fitted quietly to carry out and apply for themselves, although under the eyes of the parents at home, what they learned in the institution. In this way will suitable occupation for children influencing the life of the child, as a whole, enter the families. But in the families themselves, as a whole, true associated family life, which is in itself as elevating as it is rejuvenating, will be again formed by the new, uniting, instructive, and hence entertaining, things which the children bring home from this institution of nurture and employment. This reformation will be further aided by the sympathy which (according to experience) they will find in the parental and family circle, and thus the family will become again the temple and sanctuary for the nurture and preservation of pure human life. And this will be made sure because the several families would unite themselves in this associated [*gemeinsam*—describes what is done for a mass or collective whole rather than for a single individual—hence a school] nurture of life, and bring together their children as if to a genuine family festival.

Therefore we make this precise, clear, well-established proposition, and—according to the well-weighed facts lying before us, and the needs of the children, parents, and families, as well as of the collective whole of the relations of life, clearly recognized and proved by us—we most earnestly summon all to the accomplishment of this plan. Our plan is this, namely, that first of all, in the cities best adapted to the purpose, families already united in themselves and by their nature, inspired by the same genuine love and care for their children, feeling themselves humanly connected with each other, having a reciprocal human respect for one another, may also by association form societies for the establishment of institutions which have for their aim and the point of union of their collective life the careful preservation and harmonious development of their children, especially by fostering their impulse for activity in a manner worthy of humanity. The beneficial results, the blessings of such institutions for the domestic as well as for the public life, for the life of the citizen as well as for that of common humanity, would be quite incalculable, and would develop endlessly. For all that has now been done as well in public life as in private associations and families for the fostering care of childhood; for the observation, development and guidance of the children in their first years of life and up to the proper age for school, suits as little the present state of human development, the present state of social and civil life, as it suits the present state of human knowledge or the advance of science, of art, and of the trades. And it is so limited in respect to the true comprehension of the totality of human life, in regard to the means of development, education and training which are at our command, that the necessary means must be sought to provide what is more satisfactory for the guidance of children from their first childhood up to the commencement of the school period. But this means is simply the voluntary association of like-minded families to form *organizations* in order to afford a system of nurture adapted to the guidance and employment of those of their children who are not yet fit for school—in short, to give such children all that which they must require in accordance with their nature; and, indeed, what the parents must demand for them, in conformity with the needs of the present life.

As now the situation of all the relations of life, with the greatest earnestness, calls upon families to form such united organizations for the associated (*gemeinsam*) guardianship and guidance of their younger children, brought together for the purpose at least for a few hours of the day; we recognize also the duty on our part to work with them with all our powers, and to lend them a helping hand in carrying out these organizations by elaborating and presenting the means best adapted to the object, as well as by training for it the requisite directors and teachers. It therefore not only lies in the aim of this joint undertaking on account of the high importance of the object, but it even makes an essential part of it to call into life an institution for the education or preparation of teachers trained for the care of childhood. This should be founded here at the same time with it—in accordance with the needs repeatedly expressed to us for the purpose often indicated, namely, the observation of the life of children, and the preparation of teachers through this observation, and especially through fostering their tendency to creative activity and play—in other word, their impulse to constantly busy themselves. Therefore this would be a training school in which leaders and educators can directly have charge of a number of children in the period before the school age, and for the inculcation of the first elements and instruction of sense-perception. We will therefore willingly impart the necessary information to parents, and especially to large associations of families that may be inclined not only to take into earnest consideration the ideas here expressed, but also to carry them out. We would explain in this connection that we have entered into association with women and men who love children and childhood for the satisfactory and comprehensive execution of this design. We have a sufficient number of children of suitable age, and, in addition to this, the means required. The locality chosen for the institution is situated in a favorable spot, surrounded by rich and beautiful scenery, and the power of a pure, human, associated effort will essentially favor the carrying out of the idea and plan.

May the idea find deeply reaching accord as well as genuine sympathy in its behalf, for the sake of the welfare of the children as well as of the families; may it benefit entire communities and the entire human race, and thus prove a blessing to the individual as well as to the whole.

6

Child and the Play

Before we give the child a new play, a new means of fostering his tendency to employment, let us seek to make ourselves familiar with the exact state of cultivation to which the little one has been raised by the means of development hitherto provided for him, and with the further requirements of this stage of cultivation. Not only what we give hereafter to the child may by such knowledge be made actually to exert a beneficial influence in his life, but also we, as conscious givers, may know what onward development is to be effected in the child in harmony with the development of his whole life by means of the gift; and the child may thus confide in us more and more, may so much the more willingly receive our gift, and so much the more compliantly take into his life. For the deep, though to the child himself unconscious, cause of angelic purity, the confidence, peace, and joy with which in his yet serene childhood he receives gifts from his parents and from all those who love him, is that he trustingly feels that they give him exactly that which for the moment is beneficial to his inner as well as to his outer life; they do not give him a hard stone instead of nourishing bread; they do not give him a poisonous serpent instead of the joyous fish which gayly plays in the water and the sun. Parents, nurses, and kindergartners should spare no effort to preserve this childish faith and confidence. Their effort should be the more strenuous because the child's feelings, are on the one hand, unconscious, unconfirmed, and unfortified, and, on the other, because precisely these unconscious feelings are soil from and in which sprout forth and grow the most beautiful blossoms and plants, the most glorious fruits of life.

But how is this result attained? Manifestly through the child's oft-repeated experience that what fatherly care and motherly love now give him is precisely what he needs for the fostering and development of his life; and furthermore, that fatherly wisdom and motherly love know how to adapt to his present condition and needs even what be falls him through chance or accident. But just as these experiences confirm faith, opposite ones destroy it. If parents offer to the child at any stage of development either what he does not then need (though it be intrinsically good and useful), or if they offer it to him in a form wherein he is unable to recognize that which has beneficial effect upon his life, they will inevitably weaken and indeed destroy (though unconsciously to the child himself) his belief that his parents bear within themselves his whole life, and that they are interested not so much in the outward aspects of that life as in the child's inner nature and its necessary requirements. Such a course of action has, moreover, other and even more injurious effects. Through the child's effort to repel that which is contrary to the needs of his life, indignation and discontent are wakened in his soul; and, on the other hand, from the fact that his normal desires are ungratified, they become inordinate and mischievous.

How many parents, nurses, and kindergartners obtain means of opposing these evil results? Most satisfactorily through a threefold and yet single glance at life. Let them first look into themselves and into their own course of development, its phenomena and requirements; let them recall their own earliest years, and their later stages of development, and look deeply into their own present life. Next, let them look as deeply as possible into the life of the child, and into what he must necessarily require for his present stage of development. Having recognized what the child needs, let them scrutinize his environment, and observe, first, what it offers and does not offer for the fulfilment of such requirements. Let them utilize all offered possibilities of meeting normal needs; and when such needs can not be met, let them recognize this fact, and show the child plainly the impossibility of their fulfilment. Finally, let them clearly recognize whatever in the child's environment tends to waken antagonism and discontent, to remove it if it be removable, and admit its defect if it be not removable.

The child is very often seeks for something without at all knowing what he seeks; in like manner he repels something without at all knowing why, for this something was dear to him, and is so still under certain conditions. Yet the child does not for this reason turn away accidentally, neither does he seek the accidental; but he seeks that which is indeed unfamiliar to him but still suited to his present stage of development. Generally, it is the novel for which he seeks, but not a novelty which has no connection with what has hitherto been, for that, should it appear, would obstruct development. He seeks the new which has developed from the old, like the bud from the branch. The child seeks a new, unexpected turn; a new, unexpected use of a thing; new, unexpected properties; new and yet unconsciously anticipated developments; a new, unexpected connection with his life; and thus, above all, a new connection of his life with that of his parents, of adults, from whom he hopes for and receives suitable life food. The child indeed seeks for the new that is outside of himself, but not on account of its externality. Really he is seeking the new, of which he feels premonitions *in himself* in his own development. Since, however, he does not yet know this and so can not give an account of it, the child seeks especially for *change*, in order, as has already been intimated, to gain a means of growing up within himself and of growing forth outwardly from himself.

Above all, therefore, it is the old within the child which clarifies, unfolds, and transmutes itself, thus developing that which is new. The whole process takes place according to a definite law resting in the child himself, in his life, in life as such. Hence it is that child unconsciously (yet for this very reason positively) demands that not only all may unfold around him according to definite laws, but that this external development shall make known to him its law, and thus the law of his own life, the union or opposition of the two, and consequently the higher relatively of life.

But for the attainment of all this it is, as already stated, necessary that educators should always carry in themselves, as a whole, the course of development, the course of cultivation of the child.

But now how has the child developed up to this point?

How have the world, the objects, and things around him developed?

How has the child developed himself, especially through the means of play and employment which have thus far been given to him?

The brightening light in the child's mind illuminates the objects around him. In proportion, therefore, as the inner light increases, the nature of external objects grows clear to him. In proportion as he perceives in his own life a definite course of development, and recognizes it as a law of development—in proportion as he perceives in his own life a process of development—he will recognize a process of development in things around him. In proportion as he learns to reason from effect to cause and from cause to effect within himself, will he recognize causality in the external world. In proportion as he recognizes within himself that the *course* of development indicates a *law* of development, will he recognize this law in its external manifestations. This process and law of development is no other than that of progression from the unlimited to the limited, from the general to the special, from the unity to individuality, from embryonic to structural life, from the whole to the part, from an undifferentiated to a membered totality.

In conformity with this law the child has been educated up to this point through the gifts already considered; for the education which brings peace and blessing to children and to human beings in general is that which early suggests the truth that the outer world in its essence does not hinder but helps the life of the soul. Such help, however, is realized only in proportion as the inner and outer worlds are comprehended in their essence, their destiny, and their polar opposition. Thus understood, the outer world not only corresponds wholly to the requirements of the inner world, but even comes to meet them, and represents the inner world in and through itself.

The man advanced in insight should be as clear as possible in his own mind about all this before he introduces his pupil or his child into the outer world. Even when he gives the child a plaything he must make clear to himself its purpose, and the purpose of playthings and occupation material in general. This purpose is, to aid the child to freely express what lies within him—to bring phenomena of the outer world nearer to him, and thus to serve as mediator between the mind and the world.

Recognizing the mediatorial character of play and playthings, we shall no longer be indifferent either to the choice, the succession, or the organic connection of the toys we give to children. In those I offer them I shall consider as carefully as possible how the child may, in using them, unfold his nature freely and yet in accordance with law, and how through such use he may also learn to apprehend external things correctly and employ them justily.

As the child's first consciousness of self was born of physical opposition to and connection with the external world, so through the play with the ball the external world itself began to rise out of chaos and assume definiteness. In recognizing the ball the child moved from the indefinite to the definite, from the universal to the particular, from mere externality to a self-included, space-filling object. In the ball, especially through the *movement*, through the opposites of rest and motion, through departing and returning, the object came forth out of general space as a special space-filling object, as a *body*; just as the child, by means of his life, also perceives himself, his corporeal frame, as a space-filling object, as a *body*. The child has thus obtained two important terms of comparison for his first intellectual development: body and body, object and object. But just on that account it is by no means unimportant what kind of an object, what kind of a body is given to the child for comparison—that is, for play and playing. He feels and perceives *himself* as *life*; so he may and does perceive the ball at least, outside of himself in motion and as *motion*.

At the same time there begins in the child, as in a seed-corn, a development advancing toward manifoldness. For this reason he should receive a corresponding seed-corn in the object which he first detaches as object from the external chaos. Such object should, like himself, include an indefinite manifoldness, and be susceptible of a progressive development. Such an object is the ball.

The second gift consists of a sphere and cube, and illustrates the idea of self-opposed unity. Through the simplest of contrasting forms it calls the child's attention to differences of form. In the sphere is accentuated unity of form, yet it has the three dimensions of space and contains the possibility of the threefold division which the cube makes outwardly manifest. Thus the sphere illustrates the undeveloped unity of form; the cube, the differentiation of form. The second gift, moreover, retains and develops the movableness already illustrated with the ball, and, what is particularly interesting, develops it chiefly through exercises with the very body (the cube) which in its form embodies the idea of rest.

In the cube, divided once through the middle parallel with its sides in all three directions, and so into eight parts, *each* of the qualities of the whole or principal cube is shown *eight times* (achtmal); thus requiring (as we before explained this numerical word), to rightly consider (achten) [one of Froebel's etymologies or puns] each of these qualities. Thus the three different kinds of inner directions (surface, edge, and corner direction) come forth very remarkably by means of the divided cube; but, above all, the *three principal directions*, the three surface directions which stand at right angles to each other. These three directions, however, are still undistinguished by difference of dimension, and no inner variety is brought to light. Hence, *by* and *through* them, each can be placed in the position of the other. Through the building and grouping of these eight component cubes, however, there is temporarily manifest a difference between the three principal directions standing at right angles to each other, as *length, breadth,* and *height* (or as length, breadth, and thickness), but as abiding properties determining the form these differences of dimension are still lacking.

Hence a new gift is demanded—a gift wherein the length, breadth, and thickness of a solid body shall be distinguished from each other by difference of size. Such a gift will open the child's eyes to the three dimensions of space, and will serve also as a means of recognizing and interpreting the manifold forms and structures with which he is constantly brought in contact. Such a gift is the cube divided into eight equal oblong prisms or parallelopipeds. This is, therefore, the fourth gift of the means of plays and employment, which now follows. Through this gift the child receives a fixed measure both for permanent and vanishing forms, and thus he is able to produce a richer variety of figures and to recognize them in the forms which surround him. Hence the new gift corresponds both to his increasing constructive ability, and to his growing capacity to comprehend the external world.

We beg those parents and friends who have attentively followed us up to this point in the presentation of our means of employment for children to pause here a moment, in order to notice the simplicity and certainty with which the process of development that has been recognized as true is followed out, and the conditions of the satisfactory human education fulfilled.

One of the fundamental principles of such a process of development is that each object given must condition the one which follows; each new gift fulfills and interprets its predecessor, by making explicit what it implied. The child must receive no new gift which was not suggested by that which preceded it, neither must we require of him anything not conditioned by his previous achievements. Both these requirements find themselves wholly fulfilled in the sequence of gifts furnished up to this point, as has been already definitely shown in many point of view in the foregoing pages.

Another requirement of a satisfactory human education is this: that each object shall appear to the child as a self-included whole, and at the same time, through a many-sided connection, as a part of a greater whole. This requirement is also met clearly in a each of the means of play hitherto furnished; each is in itself a complete whole; each stands in active connection with those which precede and follow it; each bear them partially within itself, presents them from itself, and can develop them.

Another fundamental idea is, that all knowledge and comprehension of life are connected with making the internal external, the external internal, and with perceiving the harmony and accord of both. As the sphere (and still more the cube), makes more and more externally perceptible its own internal being, and that of other objects (for example, middle and directions, etc.), so, on the other hand, the child through its use learns to recognize both its own internal characteristics and the internal characteristics of external objects in general, and through such recognitions rises into knowledge of the world and of himself.

What a quiet, clear advance in the development of the child, as well as in the unfolding of the outer world, is thus given! How would it be possible to render prominent on all sides even an intimation of it in its particulars?

The Cube Divided into Eight Building Blocks—The Fourth Gift of the Series—Its Nature

Plaything and play receive a quite new significance by the above given alteration, which is not only simple but even almost insignificant—namely, that the inner difference, intimated in the three perpendicular axes of the cube (and the sphere), now becomes externally visible and abiding in each of its building blocks as a difference of size.

While the forms produced with the preceding gift were massive and space-filling, those produced with the fourth gift incline toward surface forms, may be given either a horizontal or vertical position, and are space-bounding and inclosing.

These forms are also divided into *forms of life*, of *beauty*, and of *knowledge*. Especially in comparison with the forms of the preceding play, the latter have the peculiarity that they show more the extension of surface and length; yet all forms—a few square surface excepted—are confined to rectangles. Thus the relations of form and size of the square and rectangle especially are here presented to the perception. In addition to these, two more new phenomena come forth with this play: these are *equilibrium* and self-propagating *movement*.

Use of the Play

Necessity, accident, or, in short, free play as such, receives here also its due. The only requirement is that a *name* be quickly given to what has originated under the hand of child. The name defines the object produced by connecting it with something familiar. Thus the first forms are often a *small house*, a *room*, a *table, chairs* and *benches*, etc. But pleasure is given even by merely building up the blocks so that the form may be kept in place by equilibrium and gravity; and it is then a high *tower*, or perhaps the staircase, which pleases the child. He is also pleased by the fact that what is built up separates easily into its parts again. Let no one doubt that the child's inner development is furthered by these building exercises, though no abiding result in the way of outward representation is obtained. By this building the child comprehends the form and use of the single part just in proportion as he receives into himself an abundance of perceptions and conceptions. We must, however, never forget to talk with the child about what he does, or at least designate the result clearly and precisely, with suitable words, so that through the name the child's thought may be aroused, and he may never play heedlessly even when he plays alone. In other words, let us form such habits of attention that the child will never play without precisely grasping and comprehending inwardly what he has outwardly represented.

As all representations are connected with an inner precise *condition*, so here. This condition is simply that before expressed, that for every representation, whether simple or compound, whether the parts are connected or separate (as, for example, a monument, a garden wall, or a village), *all* the blocks should be used, or, at least, be put in connection with the form. The aim of this condition also, as has been already clearly stated, is manifold: firstly, that the child should *not* busy himself *thoughtlessly*, but should have in view a *definite aim* for his action, or at least be incited to perceive an aim; secondly, that he should view the object to be represented in *many-sided references* and connections, which is necessary when, for example, an unused block is to be put in necessary connection with the object already represented; thirdly, and *lastly*, that the child *should employ all the material before him, and leave nothing unconsidered and unused*. Through fulfilling these conditions the child develops on the one hand his power of perception and conception, and on the other the more spiritual powers of fantasy and inner contemplation.

We have above stated that necessity, accident, or free play determines the first use of the new gift. We will now indicate the next thing to be done. The mother takes the play-box, reverses it, placing it with the cover on the table, draws out the cover from under the box and raises up the latter, so that the cube stands before the child. The representations may be most satisfactorily made on a board or paper provided with a square network, each side of the square being of the same size or length as the width of a building block. The mother transforms the cube, as she speaks, into a fireplace in the kitchen, at which she prepares the soup for the hungry child and cooks the food for the father when he comes from his work. The fire burns *in the middle* of the fireplace, *on* the fire-iron. One can go round the fire-place in order to poke the fire better, in order to cook the food more carefully.

The soup is ready, the food is cooked. The mother and child give the fireplace a push, and it separates into stones for building. The fireplace *consists of building stones* of equal size.

The child wants the soup. The father comes; he desires to eat, but there is no table. The material is immediately changed; the building stones become *building blocks*, or boards, and there stands the *table*. But the *bench* is now lacking; the *chairs*, the *benches* are wanted, so that the mother, with the child and the father, may sit down to eat. The table is generally too large, and one-half it (or rather one-half of its material) is quickly changed to a bench or to two such benches. On the one bench the father sits and eats his food; on the other the mother sits with the child and gives it its soup.

Again, the fireplace is separated into parts; the material does not change. It is summer; it is a beautiful warm evening. The child plays in the yard at the stone table or on the stone benches. The father comes and sits down by the child; the mother brings him his food and the child its soup. On the bench at the right the father sits; upon the one at the left the mother sits with the child. The mother tells the father how nicely the child has played, how quietly he has occupied himself with his blocks, and thus given her time to prepare the food. The father brings the child a beautiful blue flower from the field. "See, dear child, here is the flower."

Or, again, another time the stone table and benches are viewed as a turf-table and benches; they stand now, not in the yard but in the garden. When the father hears that the child has pleased his mother, he goes and picks for him the beautiful red flower which nodded to him so kindly.

As two benches were formed from the one-half of the large table, so two more benches are now made from the other half. In the middle of the garden is a round plate; around this stand *four benches turned toward it*. See! five little children are playing "Rooms to let." One child asks now of one, now of another, "Is there no room to be had?" "No chamber to let?" "Is no place open?" "All are occupied." See! there two neighbors change places, and the questioner has quickly taken the place of one of them.

Another time the children play "Visiting." Each of the benches or seats becomes a little house. Or, again, the child builds itself a little house or open garden-hut. Visits are paid or received; or the mother sits with the child in one corner. Either she tells him something about the carpenter or joiner who has built the house of boards and laths, and made it so strong that they can sit in it quietly, or the tired child sleeps in the mother's arms or on her lap, and she sings to him a little slumber-song:

The child has tired itself of play;
Its eyelids droop at close of day;

It lies upon its mother's breast,
To children a sweet place of rest,
Willingly—yes, willingly!

Another time, the mother goes to walk with the child in the garden; but the wind blows strongly, the rain beats down; so she hurries with the child into the "opened garden-hut." That has doors, which the mother can shut. Now both are safe, for the hut has a roof, so that it can not rain in, and doors, so that the wind can not drive the rain in.

In like manner, if some manifestation of the child gives occasion thereto, the fact may be brought out that the wooden benches and chairs have backs, but the stone and turf benches have none.

It is quite important for the child, and it greatly pleases him, to notice how one object springs from another, and can be turned into another; for example, a table into a table and *two* benches; these into *four* benches, etc. Through such transformations "the bench with high back and arms" may be produced from the throne; from this bench may be made the bench with back, arms, and foot-rest; from this, again, the open garden-hut, etc. This changing one thing into another, and so being able to see one in another, is what gives the children pleasure and brings life into their employment and play. The anticipation of a certain necessary inner coherence in the thing, whether it be in its form or in its purpose—this manifold perception of a certain inner life throughout—not only awakens, but fosters and forms the life of the child. Isolation and exclusion destroy life; union and participation create life.

But living objects also may be represented with the blocks; for example, "six blocks form an avenue; father and mother, brothers or sisters, go to walk in it." Another time, "two blocks, laid one on another, with their broad sides touching, form a cow, or one standing alone, a calf; in the same manner, three or more blocks form a horse and its colt; two blocks joined like a cross represent a herdsman"—thus the child has the herd and herdsman. Then the herd may be driven in, and *presto*, change, six blocks from the stable with two stalls; the two remaining blocks are two cows, etc.

These representations are, indeed, not found on the lithograph leaves, but we indicate them up here in order to show how life itself may be connected with and represented by inanimate objects. The scope of this work makes it unwise to enter into further detail with regard to the *life forms* which may be produced with the fourth gift. In the actual use of this gift with children many more forms will be produced; indeed, they have already been produced, and shall be indicated hereafter.

That the salient characteristics and organic members of the life forms may be thrown into relief by means of stories and talks we have already sufficiently shown, both in connection with this gift and with the third gift. What has been written should, however, be carefully connected with actual use of the gift, and this is especially important in those cases where a *moving force* is manifested outwardly, as equilibrium or as self-propagating activity. Self-propagating activity, moreover, may be simple or in one single direction, divided or having different directions. It may also be uniform or accelerating.

Let us now turn to a new consideration—to the observation of the forms of knowledge.

The whole eight building blocks of the fourth gift, taken collectively, resemble the cube of the third gift; therefore its parts (as can be seen at the first glance) separate into equal and proportional parts. This fact is made yet more manifest by the play with the blocks. Thus the one bench is divided into two equal benches, and the bench with the foot-rest into the two equal benches with foot-rests; likewise the table into two halves, of which the one gives again a table, while the outer half appears divided into two halves in the two chairs or benches. So, the fourth gift illustrates almost the same relations of size as the cube divided once through the middle on all sides, or, in other words, with the third gift. Should the relations of size, learned by observation and obstructed from the forms of life, be looked at purely as relations of size, they would appear in the fourth gift more as relations of surface and its extension, while with the third gift they appeared as extension of solids and as relations of solids.

The "high wall", which one can think of when lying on the horizontal surface as a "floor" and can actually place thus before the child, makes the easiest transition from forms of life to forms of *knowledge*. The treatment of these forms has been already shown in general in the illustrative exercise with the third gift. The fourth gift , however, throws into relief the perception of size by showing similarity of size with dissimilarity of dimension and position. For example, the gift as a whole may be shown first as a cube, then as a tablet. Changes such as these between the representations of solids and surfaces give the fourth gift a peculiar charm for the child:

As *cube* I stand here in my place;
As *surface* now, I show my face,
Yet always am the same—
I like this pretty game.
Now without delay
Divide me in your play;
Making fleetly,
But yet neatly,
Two quite equal parts.

While the mother or kindergartner sings this [or some better] rhyme, she divides the whole cube by *one* motion into two equal parts. The division may be made either vertically or horizontally. In both cases the result is the production of two square prisms, the positions of which vary according to the manner of division. While the mother represents these, she sings in the person of the square to the child:

From above if you divide me,
Both the halves will be upright;
Straight across if you divide me,
Halves recumbent meet your sight.
In position not the same;
But in size they are the same,
Each is like the other half.

If one now wishes to represent more strikingly to the child that the size and form remain the same in different positions, one places the halves with their broad sides now upon one another, thus doubling their height; now side by side, thus doubling their length. In both cases the action is interpreted by song:

Place one half upon one half,
The form is high, we see.
Lay one half beside one half,
A long form this must be;
Yet equal form and size do show
In each position, as we know.

The upright rectangle may also be turned by degrees on the horizontal plane, as it were, around its middle, or like the hand of a clock or watch around one of its ends, till it assumes the horizontal position.

Whether I am high or low,
Equal form and size I show.

Then different form with equal size:

Place one half *before* a half,
It shows the square complete.

Place the half *beside* the half,
And an oblong shape we meet.

Though different the forms may be,
An *equal size* in each we see.

That objects identical in form and size may be produced in different ways may also be illustrated in the play with the fourth gift. The child's attention should be called to all these features of his play as *perceptible* facts, and nothing should be passed over heedlessly.

Place a half *beside* a half,
It shows the *square* complete.

Place a half *before* a half,
A *square* form still we meet.

Though made in different ways, 'tis clear
Equal the *size* and *form* appear.

A new variation of these exercises may be made by dividing the square prism into two equal halves and giving to one a vertical, to the other a horizontal position. The two may then be compared with one another:

> Now I will give you something new,
> Something you will like to do:
> *Twice* as long and *half* as wide,
> *Half* as long and *twice* as wide,
> *The same size* are we two.

From this representation of the whole as a square tablet, from halving it in two different ways, and from the different possible combinations of these halves, it is evident that the fourth gift offers a far greater number of forms of knowledge than its predecessor. The plates illustrating this gift show a much greater variety of forms than is indicated in the text; and in the description of the gift others will be mentioned. The hints here given suffice to show that the forms of knowledge are adapted to children of three and four years of age, and that they incite plays which are both spontaneous and nourishing to heart and intellect. Yet more than has been here presented is represented by the tablet itself, and yet more is rendered prominent by the description of the play. Yet these few indications for the use of the forms of knowledge as play must here suffice; for they already show with quite sufficient clearness how their contemplation and comprehension are perfectly suited to the life, mind, and spirit of children three and four years of age, and so wholly adapted to actual free play which forms both spirit and heart. The comprehension and treatment of the gift by the motherly spirit, and the representations and perceptions to which such treatment gives rise, will impart to the play a life it is impossible to indicate by the lifeless word. When, however, the word and play are used to throw light upon each other, the exercise is refreshing, elevating, and life-giving. Such exercises, moreover, give the child a presentiment of the inner harmony of Nature and life. To lead to comprehension of this harmony is, in a certain sense, the true aim of education.

We now turn to the consideration of *forms* of *beauty*, or *picture forms*, or, as they might be called in a figurative sense, *harmonious forms*; and perhaps this name might also have its good and its developing effect, since it is certainly acknowledged that the true comprehension of a thing proceeds especially from its connection with its opposite; thus, in the case, from the connection of the visible and the audible, of quiescence and movement.

The transition to the forms of beauty (picture forms, or, as we have just called them, harmonious forms) is most suitably effected through the forms of knowledge. We consider it very important to retain this transition in general, and more especially in the life and play with the still quite small children.

Now, if each of these four members is turned into the opposite position, so that the corner of each square or member comes to lie where its side lay before, and thus appears as an opposite square, and the corners touch at the same time, the whole becomes still more definitely a form of beauty.

If, now, each of these four members is further separated into two, and thus the whole four members into eight, and they enter in this way into symmetrical reference to the invisible but nevertheless determining middle, the unity and (by the connecting greater manifoldness) the inner beauty of the whole are rendered yet more prominent. But this, again, conditions a double variety: either the broad sides are turned toward the middle, or the end surfaces. In the latter case the form appears *radiate*; in the former case, *circular* or inclosing. These forms are counterparts.

The appearance of forms which are at once antithetic and related calls for mediation or transition from one to the other. Hence the radiate form must be connected by intermediate forms with the circular. Such connecting forms are of two kinds: in one kind the radiate form is within the circular; in the other it is outside the circular. These transitional forms demand a fresh mediation; hence the figure where the radiate from both contains and is contained by the circular.

But now what takes place with the building blocks, when they rest on their *broad* faces as in the cases indicated, takes place also when they are placed on their *long*, narrow faces, and appears again when they stand upright on their ends. Each change of position gives rise to five new forms, and thus fifteen forms are produced by placing the blocks first on their broadest faces, next on their long, narrow faces, and finally on end. If these three different kinds of position are connected among themselves, over a hundred new and constantly differing forms may be by degrees produced in the course of fostering the child's impulse to development, and can be represented by him. For child-life gives time and opportunity enough for this. So originates a blissful filling up of many hours which were before unemployed by the children; or, at least employed in unmeaning and worthless activity, since in each individual form, and yet more in each particular series of forms, lie laws of life, of Nature, and in general of formation, which in that course of the development of the human being enter into his consciousness in the comparison with Nature and life.

We must now glance at another consideration, differing from the preceding, but not less fruitful for child and play as well as for the adult playmate.

If we survey the forms of beauty produced with the fourth gift in their totality and in connection with the unity from which they are developed—if, in order to attain yet greater unity, we compare them with the forms of beauty produced with the third gift—it strikes the eye very significantly that all these forms and structures rest inclosed, wrapped up, as it were, in the form of beauty of the third gift as in a bud. The first comparing glance at this, and also at the remaining forms of the plate, shows how all forms are conditioned—one might say contained.

In and through what characteristic of the fourth gift is grounded the vast number of different forms which proceed from the single germinal form A? It is not because the *three* principal dimensions of space, which in the cube only make themselves known as differences of position in the fourth gift, become more prominent, and manifest themselves as differences of *size*? These three relations of *size* are in the fourth gift as abiding and changeless as the *position* of the three principal direction was before and still is.

If we now admit that every one of the forms of beauty produced with the fourth gift may be regarded and used as fundamental form, we can perceive what a number of forms of beauty (scarcely calculable, and yet more difficult to survey at a glance) may be produced with this gift, and how, nevertheless, the conditions for the representation of each longer or shorter series may always be given in the most exact and definite manner. To illustrate: We may require the child to produce either forms whose sides are all equal, or again forms whose sides are unequal. Confining our attention to the former class, we observe that these may be either encircling, radiate, or made up of the two. Restricting ourselves again to his third variety of figures, we may still further narrow our activity by requiring that the component blocks be placed either on their largest, smallest, or intermediate faces. Finally, each of these forms is susceptible of manifold alteration. Hence the fourth gift combines universality, boundlessness, and freedom, with restriction and limitation. In this play, indeed, law and coherence emerge even from the apparently capricious and accidental, for, by following the path of development indicated, each particular form appears as a member of a relatively higher and more inclusive unity, until finally all forms are related to the germinal form. In the visible connection of the pure antitheses lies the formative and instructive influence of this gift for the child. The child early anticipates, perceives, and recognizes how intimately the finite and infinite, necessity and freedom, law, and free will are connected with one another; how inner limitations and law lie at the foundation even of accident, if we are only in condition to perceive and solve all the limitations and connecting links and combinations given at the same time in and with it.

The illustration of this universal law by means of perceptible phenomena is, in our judgement, as important for the heart and soul culture of the child as the absorption of light and color through the day, and the inhalation of air from the atmosphere.

How shall these representations of forms of beauty be carried on with the children? Precisely as has been already explained in the original delineation of these plays: in the same way as mothers play with their children, of their own accord, and guided by motherly love and motherly feeling. Mother observe some kind of a thing which they believe will captivate the child's mind, be it only for an instant, and they try forthwith to retain it for the child's observation. Some particular object which has a symmetric form has been represented by the mother or the child, or by both together. Through its symmetry it captivates for an instant the child's attention. The watchful mother perceives the fascination, and seeks to heighten and retain it through words spoken or sung—e.g.:

This is a very pretty play,
All our blocks in a wreath to lay.

If, on another occasion, the accidentally originated form should be one of those represented, the mother might throw it into clearer relief by singing or saying:

Now all our blocks toward the middle go,
And clearly a beautiful star they show.

Occasionally forms are produced which, though symmetrical, are not alike on all their sides. Thus the reader will remember that with the third gift were produced forms whose opposite side were equal but whose adjacent sides were unequal. Such figures as these must be interpreted by words calling attention to the positions of the sides and the number of blocks:

Place three blocks on the left,
Place three blocks on the right,
With one above and one below, the left and right unite

Any mother or kindergartner who sympathizes with the child's habits of thought may with a little experience learn to rhyme all his activities and their results. Through her jingles she will make clear to the little one what he has done, and thus his accidental productions will become a point of departure for his self-development. Word and form are opposite, and yet related. Hence the word should always accompany the form as its shadow. In a certain sense, giving a form a name really creates the form itself. Through the name, moreover, the form is retained in memory and defined to thought.

In addition to wreath, star, and flower forms, the blocks of the fourth gift may be used to produce wheel forms. These wheels forms are transitional or mediate the forms of beauty and the forms of life. This transitional or mediatorial character should be indicated to the child, and through this and similar experiences he should be given a presentiment of the truth that in all the phenomena of life there is a connection of antitheses of mediation of opposites. An early foreboding of this truth is, on our judgement, of the highest importance to the true development of each human being, for thereby all the phenomena of life are connected into living and life-giving whole, and nothing remains isolated and insignificant.

The fourth gift has now been considered in sufficient detail, and its practical use indicated in the three essential directions [forms of life, knowledge, beauty]. Two points, however, needs further consideration: First, the play itself and the adult playmate; second, the relationship and connection of the different gifts.

The Play and the Adult Playmate

How rich is the material afforded by this fourth gift for spiritual and intellectual activity, for correct apprehension of the life of childhood, and for the development of that life, has been so clearly indicated in the preceding pages that it need not further be dwelt upon. Nothing of abiding importance for the human being is untouched by it. It throws light upon life and Nature, touches the springs of feeling and thought, incites action and achievement. It illustrates the laws and conditions of human development, reveals its inner spirit, illuminates its outer manifestations, and throws into relief its successive stages.

Thus it leads to the attainment of the peace of life and of the joy of life. It elevates the family into the guardianship of peace and the promotion of happiness, for through it means are given by which all that has living worth may be drawn within the circle of family activities. Hence to the thoughtful adult this little play may become a mirror which reflects the essential law of life; a point of departure and comparison, through which the phenomena of life may be interpreted; a bridge, which shall connect the inner being of the child with external phenomena, and conversely shall interpret external phenomena to the heart and imagination of the child. Thus our fourth gift becomes in the hands of a reflective person a wonderful means of education; for through sensible facts and experiences runs the path to heart and mind, to will and deed.

The Relation and Connection of the Different Gifts

It was pointed out, in the commentary on the second gift, that the introduction of this gift to the child should not supersede the use of its predecessor, but that, on the contrary, the two gifts should be played with alternately, the one thus assisting to produce a clearer apprehension and more varied use of the other. The same statement was made in the commentary on the third gift, and its relationship to the second gift in particular was clearly shown. It must, however, be repeated again, for the third and fourth gifts complement each other in a striking manner, and their alternate use gives new life and freshness to each, and is most strengthening and developing to the spirit of the child. Hence, if several children of about the same age (from two to four years old) are playing, some with the third and some with the fourth gift, they may occasionally exchange boxes with each other. Each child should pass his box in good condition to his neighbor. No one should be allowed to push the contents of his box in a disorderly confusion to the child with whom he exchanges gifts. This requirement is essential both to the retention of the child's respect for the plaything and to the awakening and nourishing of his own sense of order. A similar requirement must be insisted upon when the child, playing alone, wishes to change from one gift to the other. He must combine his component cubes into a large cube, place the box over this, then close and put away the box, before he is allowed to receive the new gift. Such treatment of each gift as a separate and distinct whole is especially important, because thereby the common and unifying elements of the different gifts are accentuated. In like manner, when several children are playing at the same time, with the same gift of the series, it is important that each eight blocks or bricks should have their own box. They should be taken out of this box at the beginning of the play and put back into it at the conclusion. They should never be kept in or taken from a common box or receptacle. Unimportant as these little rules may appear, they are essential to the clear and definite development of the child, to his orderly apprehension of external objects, and to the logical unfolding of his own concepts and judgements.

In a word, the play box should always be treated as a loved, esteemed, and worthy companion. These three requirements hang together.

In a word, the box of building blocks should be regarded by the child as a worthy, an appreciated, and a loved comrade. The three feelings are intimately connected.

When the child has learned to use each of the gifts separately, and has seized their essential and distinctive characteristics, he may be allowed to use them together. This joint use of his playthings is particularly important in the case of the third and fourth gifts.

Since, however, the combination of the third and fourth gifts creates an expansion of the child's play, and requires from him increased power of perception and increased creative ability, the two boxes should not be used together until their separate possibilities have been thoroughly mastered.

7

The Fifth Stage in Teaching

Before beginning his play with this gift the child must apprehend it as a symmetrical whole, complete in itself. The component cubes should be so packed in their box as to bring the divided cubes undermost; it is also essential that cubes similarity divided should be placed in a row. In conformity with this demand the bottom of the box must be occupied by one row of undivided cubes, one row of halved cubes, and row of quartered cubes. The eighteen remaining undivided cubes fill the rest of the box.

If the cubes be thus arranged in the box and covered with the lid, it is only necessary to place the box on the table with the cover downward, then to draw out the cover and raise the box with a steady hand. When the box is withdrawn the whole cube, with its parts well arranged, stands before the child.

This procedure is by no means intended merely to make the withdrawal of the box easy for the child, but, on the contrary, brings to him much inner profit. It is well for him to receive his plaything in an orderly manner—not to have them tossed to him as fodder is tossed to animals. It is good for the child to begin his play with the perception of a whole, a simple self-contained unit, and from this unity to develop his representations. Finally, it is essential that the playing child should receive his material so arranged that its various elements are discernible, and that by seeing them his mind may unconsciously from plans for using them. Receiving his material thus arranged, the child will use it with ever-recurrent and increasing satisfaction, and his play will produce for more abiding results than the play of one whose material lies before him like a heap of cobble-stones.

Since the right use of all objects, whether physical or spiritual, implies primarily division and recombination, or analysis and synthesis, according to definite aims, let the first use of the fifth gift be.

The Representation of Forms of Knowledge

The simplest of these forms of knowledge are obtained by division. The simplest form of division is that which separates the whole cube into equal parts of the least number, and having the greatest similarity in form to the whole cube. Therefore the first division of the fifth gift is into three equal square prisms.

It will be remembered that the third gift was divided in three different ways, but that the parts thus divided differed only in position. In two of these divisions the plane of division was vertical; in one it was horizontal. The two vertical planes differed by extending in one case from right to left and in the other from front to back. In the fifth gift this threefold division is repeated, and is now accompanied by variation in the arrangement of the component cubes. In other words, when the fifth gift is divided horizontally all the divided component cubes will be found in one of its thirds. When it is divided vertically from right to left, the halved cubes will be found in one of its thirds and the quartered cubes in another. When it is divided from front to back, one of the halved cubes and one of the quartered cubes will be found in each third.

Perceptions and recognitions which are with difficulty gained from *words* are easily gained from facts and deeds. Through actual experience the child gains in a trice a total concept, whereas the same concept expressed in words would be only grasped in a partial manner. The rare merit, the vivifying influence of this play material is that, through the representations it makes possible, concepts are recognized at once in their wholeness and unity, whereas such an idea of a whole can only very gradually be gained from its verbal expression. It must, however, be added that later, through words, the concept can be brought into higher and clearer consciousness. Rhythmic or harmoniously membered speech especially tends to produce this result. Hence all perceptions should be connected with words, that thereby they may be more clearly defined in thought.

Therefore the division and recombination of our cubes may be accompanied by the words—

One whole, three thirds;
Three thirds, one whole.

If, in addition to connecting the act with its interpreting word, we connect with the words the rhythmic form, then to sense-perception and intellectual apprehension we shall give the apprehension of the heart, or, in other words, we shall influence the whole nature of the child as a triune being:

1 5 5 3 1 1
One whole now, three thirds see;
1 5 5 3 1 1
Three thirds now, one whole see.

This very simple division of the cube gives occasion for a great variety of representations; the three table-shaped parts produced by the horizontal division can be joined so as to form a rectangular prism, whose greatest length may be either vertical or horizontal. In either case the rectangular prism may be again divided into three beam-shaped parts [square prisms]—i.e., in beam-shaped parts having a horizontal position, and into beam-shaped parts having a vertical position. To the child these differences of position make the beam seem as different as an oblong whose greater length is horizontal seems to him different from an oblong whose greater length is vertical. Here, again, division and recombination are accompanied by word, accent, and song:

One table—three beams;
Three beams—one table.

Again, we may consider the rectangular prism formed by uniting the three square prisms as one long table, and, as we alternately divide and reconstruct it, say—

> Long table will three small ones make;
> To form long table three small ones take.

Or, more briefly—

> Long rectangle, three squares see;
> From three squares, rectangle make for me.

In this case direct attention to upper face of prisms. Or—

> One oblong, three squares;
> Three squares, one oblong.

In this case the oblong in different positions are recognized as having the same form.

The same law must be observed here as in all other plays—the law which permits the child entire freedom in developing from a given point of departure. Thus proceeding from the rectangular prism the child may, according to his own impulse, develop the rhomboidal prism to the trapezoidal prism. These forms lead on to the hexagonal and pentagonal prisms.

In all cases, however, it is an incitement to thought and feeling if simple words and melodies are used to define the child's doings. Through such interpretation the act recoils with the more developing power—e.g.:

> My cube I can handle
> With ease, and you'll see
> Six corners, where four
> Or where five used to be.

Or—

> How easy 'tis my cube to take
> And from one form another make!

It is both edifying and enjoyable for the child to discover and repeatedly represent how one form proceeds from another by lawful evolution, as has just been illustrated in the series moving from the rectangular prism or parallelopiped to hexagonal prism. It is also important for the child to define each form in word—e.g.:

> A rectangle has four right angles, etc.;
> A rhomboid has two sharp and two blunt
> angles.

Definitions of this kind must be given without any proof, and simply as verbal expressions of perceptible facts. They should be uttered rhythmically, and should be interpreted by pointing with the fingers to the angles indicated. Thus the words, "Two sharp angles, two blunt angles," should be repeated alternately, and the angles touched as they are named.

Even these definitions may be made rhythmic:

> Scan well these forms, always four angles you will
> find,
> Yet ever different are their sides inclined.

So when the angles are similar but have different position, the following words may be said:

> Though these angles alike appear,
> In position they differ here.

[That is, the two equal angles either on different sides (rhomboid) or on the same side (trapezoid).]

In further explanation may be added the following words:

> The two that are blunt are the larger angles;
> The two that are sharp are the smaller angles.

And further:

> Blunt angles on the shorter sides we see;
> Sharp angles on the longer sides must be.

In all that is done, however, the aim must be to follow simply, quietly, and thoughtfully the requirements of the child's inner nature—an aim which these gifts make it easy to realize. The child's representations must be lifted into the clearness and precision for which he longs, and finally his productions must be clearly defined in words.

From this digression, to which we have allowed ourselves to be led as in play by the child, we return to the division of the cubes.

As the division of the cube into thirds was made in three different ways, so the third may be divided in three different ways into ninths, and these into twenty-sevenths.

Again, the component cubes may be united so as to form a rhomboidal, a pentagonal, or a hexagonal prism, and divided in several different ways into two, three, four, six, and more equal parts; the shapes of these parts will be four, five, six, and eight sided prisms. They are always, however, *right* prisms—i.e., prisms whose lateral faces form right angles with bases. The use of the cube makes these facts so apparent, that they need only be indicated for each person to discover them for himself and to lead children to discover them.

The children may be incited to effort and discovery by rhymed question and suggestion:

> Who can now the large cube change,
> And one six-sided form arrange?

Or—

> And two six-sided forms arrange.
>
> The cube can change, if each child only tries,
> To four straight rows alike in form and size.
>
> See! now I can divide all these
> Into five-sided forms with ease.
>
> Whoever can handle the cube well can change
> *These* form, and four six-sided forms can arrange.
>
> The four six-sided forms you now may take,
> And of them two eight-sided figures make.
>
> Look at me now, and lastly you shall learn
> How two eight-sided forms to one may turn.
>
> Four equal slanting lines we here can view;
> The other sides are equal two and two.
>
> This cube is very changeable; you may turn it with much ease
> To forms whose bases have five sides, and more yet, if you please.

Or—

> The cube its parts unites in different ways,
> And with each changes a different form displays.

The transformation of one from into another thrown into relief by these line is highly important in its developing influence. The forms advance from the simple to the complex and return again to the simple, thus completing a cycle of development.

In every case separation and division must be followed by recombination. In this way there result from the cube, by varied groupings of its constituent parts, prisms, whose bases have 4, 6, or 8 sides. [Froebel here describes these prisms as "four-times-one-sided, two-times-two-and-one-sided, two-and-three-times-one-sided, one-time-three-sided, once two-sided, and once one-sided, four times two-sided."] These bodies after being built up may be easily resolved into their different constituent prisms. The manner of doing this well be perceived at a glance.

A very delightful exercise is to discover how many square prisms may be made of the twenty-seven cubes. Such square prisms may be, first, all of equal size; second, all of different sizes; third, part of equal and part of unequal sizes. Analogous exercises may be carried out with the pentagonal and hexagonal solids. Here as everywhere the point of prime importance for its formative influence is the development of one form from another.

Let us illustrate this kind of exercise by the example of the square prism.

First. Equal Square Prisms.

Of these there are three, each composed of nine cubes.

Second. Unequal Square Prisms.

Two Square Prisms.

1 of 25 and 1 of 2 cubes.
1 of 18 and 1 of 9 cubes.

Three Square Prisms.

1 of 16, 1 of 9, 1 of 2 cubes.

Four Square Prisms.

1 of 16, 1 of 8, 1 of 2, 1 of 1 cube.

Five Square Prisms.

1 of 16, 1 of 4½, 1 of 4, 1 of 2, 1 of ½ cube

Third. Equal and Unequal Square Prisms.

Three Square Prisms.

1 of 25 cubes, 2 of 1 cube each.

Four Square Prisms.

2 of 9 cubes each, 2 of 4½ cubes each.
2 of 9, 1 of 8 cubes, 1 of 1 cube.
1 of 16, 2 of 4½ cubes, 1 of 2 cubes.

Five Square Prisms.

1 of 16, 2 of 4½ cubes each, 2 of 1 cube each.
1 of 16, 1 of 8, 1 of 2 cubes, 2 of ½ cube each.
2 of 9, 1 of 4½, 1 of 4 cubes, 1 of ½ cube.

Six Square Prisms.

2 of 9, 1 of 4½, 2 of 2 cubes each, 1 of ½ cube.

Seven Square Prisms.

1 of 9, 1 of 8, 1 of 4, 2 of 2 cubes each, 2 of 1 cube each.
2 of 4½, 4 of 4, 1 of 2 cubes.

Eight Square Prisms.

1 of 9, 1 of 8, 1 of 4, 1 of 2 cubes, 4 of 1 cube each.
1 of 4½, 5 of 4, 1 of 2 cubes, 1 of ½ cube.
6 of 4, 1 of 2 cubes, 1 of 1 cube.

Nine Square Prisms.

1 of 9, 1 of 8, 1 of 4, 1 of 2 cubes, 3 of 1 cube, 2 of ½ cube.

Ten Square Prisms.

5 of 4, 3 of 2 cubes, 2 of ½ cube.

Eleven Square Prisms.

4 of 4, 4 of 2 cubes each, 3 of 1 cube each.

Twelve Square Prisms.

5 of 4 cubes each, 7 of 1 cube each, etc.

We have illustrated in perhaps exhaustive detail the square prisms which may be made at the same time from the component cubes of the fifth gift. For this procedure I have had two reasons: first, to give a sample of the great number of instructive forms which this gift makes possible; second, to show what beautiful combinations proceed from these forms.

Of these combinations two are as follows:

I. Place two or more square prisms one above the other, taking care that the superimposed prism is just half the size of the one upon which it rests: e.g., upon a square prism formed of eighteen component cubes place one of nine cubes; upon a square prism of sixteen component cubes place one of eight, upon this one of four, then in order one of two cubes, one of one cube, and one of one half cube.

If, now, a series of these diminishing square prisms or tablets be laid one upon another, in such a way that the angles of one tablet always touch the sides of its predecessor, the structure resulting will be both pretty and instructive.

Again, if while thus arranging the tablets each tablet be defined relatively to its predecessor as its *opposite* (because of the contrast in position), the fact will impress itself upon the mind that each *opposite* tablet is precisely half the size of the preceding or principal tablet to which it refers. Analogous observations may of course be made in many ways, and in a later stage of development receive accurate expression in geometry. As illustrated with our gift it is a mere experience reached through play, and relates to simple perception of a composite whole, together with the agreeable impression of this whole upon the eye, and through the eye upon the feeling and disposition.

The following words, which must be connected with contrasting observations (i.e., observation of the form from below upward, and from above downward), will make the relative sizes of the different tablets clear to the child:

Upward, always half as large;
Downward, always twice as large.

Or, with each single tablet--

I'm twice as large as that above me,
And half as large as that below;
But though twofold I appear,
One you'll always find me here.

The second combination alluded to, and which is not less interesting than the one already considered, is as follows: Unite two equal square prisms by their edges (or corners) so that their upper surfaces from a right angle, and connect these prisms by a third square prism extending from the free edge of one to the free edge of the other. This third square prism will contain as many cubes as both the two forms originally united—e.g.:

Unite two cubes by their edges to form a right angle; the connecting square prism will contain four cubes.

Unite square prisms of four cubes each; the connecting square prism will contain eight cubes.

Unite square prisms of four cubes and a half each; the connecting square prism will contain nine cubes.

Unite square prisms of eight cubes each; the connecting square prism will contain sixteen cubes.

Unite square prisms of nine cubes each; the connecting square prism will contain eighteen cubes, etc.

If desired, this process may be described in rhyme:

> Let two equal square prisms in a right angle meet,
> The prism formed is twice as large when it is quite complete.

If one desires that the explanatory word shall accompany each stage of the representation (by which means word, act, and object become reciprocally explanatory and vitalizing), the following line may be used:

> If you can by an edge unite
> Two equal squares with an angle right,
> And by a third square can combine
> Two other edges of these squares in line,
> This last third square will, as you plainly see,
> As large as both the others prove to be.

For the further development of this group of forms we must refer to the complete direction for the use of this gift.

It need here only be added that the discovery and combination of geometric forms other than square prisms is also full of interest, and that the mathematical relationships thrown into relief in such combinations are most interesting and instructive. The combinations of hexagonal prism may be mentioned as peculiarly attractive.

Up to this point the child has been incited to discover figures of like form but of different content. He may now be led to discover figures having an equal cubic content but dissimilar in form—e.g.:

First Series

1. A square prism of four cubes.
2. A prism with trapezoidal base, of four cubes.
3. A prism (whose bases are isosceles triangle) of for cubes.

[It will be understood that *half* cubes are used in making the last two forms.]

Second Series

4. A square prism two cubes long, one cube wide.
5. A rhomboidal prism of similar length and width.
6. A prism whose bases are isosceles triangles, made of one whole and two half cubes, each of its legs or lateral sides being of the length of two cubes, and one of these sides serving as its base.

Third Series

7. One Small cube.
8. One square tablet of four cubes.
9. One right column whose bases are one inch square and whose height is four inches.

A single observation brings to light the following facts:

1. Two parallel-sided quadrangles having like bases are equal, if of the same height.

> Whatever form the two sided show,
> Slanting or straight, or high or low,
> If base and height alike you see,
> The contents too will equal be.

2. Any parallel-sided quadrangular form and a prism whose bases are isosceles triangles are of equal size when with the same altitude the base of the latter [i.e., of the triangle] is twice as large as the base of the former [i.e., of the quadrangle].

> Four corners *you* can bring to view,
> While only three *I* show to you;
> And see now—I am just as tall
> As you; and yet that is not all,
> For I can cover twice the ground:

Our contents equal thus are found.

The figures of the second series when compared with one another throw into relief the first of the above-mentioned facts. Again, the *quadrangular* figures of the second when compared with the quadrangular figures of the first series show that one parallelogram has half of the contents of another when with equal base it has half the altitude. The rhyme for this is easily discovered.

The equality of the triangle of this series with its parallelograms may be thus expressed:

Four corners you can bring to view,
While only three I show to you.
Twice as tall I am as you,
Just as long, and it is true
That, as we cover equal ground,
Our contents equal must be found.

The triangle of the second series compared with that of the first series shows that one triangle is half the size of another when with half the base it has an equal altitude.

In the third series the bases of the two square prisms show—

1. Proceeding from the smaller to the larger:

When the base and altitude of one square prism are equal to one-half the base and altitude of another, its cubic contents are only-fourth as great.

2. Proceeding from the larger to the smaller:

When the base and altitude of one square prism are twice as great as the base and altitude of another, the cubic contents of the former are four times as great as those of the latter.

The mathematical truths shown in this third series were also presented to perception in the third gift, but repeated experiences are of great profit to the child.

The transition from these forms of knowledge to forms

---

* The child also loves to build kitchen and cellar, incited thereto, perhaps, by the fascination of the hidden and mysterious.

of beauty and forms of life is a very simple one. It will, however, not be readily discoverable by children, who will, on the contrary, begin at once with forms of life.

Forms of Life

The one permanent and indispensable condition in the production of these forms of life is that in each total product all that material of the gift shall be used. Any piece that is left over must be somehow placed in relation to the whole, and appear as an essential member of the collective representation. Closely following the inclination of the child, we too will now begin with the forms of life;* and this so much the more, because the manifestations of the child show that through life and deed he is led to the consideration and representation of the beautiful and the true; and, again, that it is the apprehension of the beautiful which leads to consideration, representation, and apprehension of the true. The child, in a word, follows the same path as the man, and advances from use to beauty, and from beauty to truth.

In presenting this gift I have, however, purposely given the precedence to the forms of knowledge. My object is to make parents and kindergartners familiar with nature of the gift and its possible mathematical combinations. In proportion as the leader is thoroughly acquainted with the material of the gift will be the profit of the plays to which he or she will incite the child, and the pleasure of such plays both to leader and child.

With regard to the production of forms of life the same principle holds good as in the production of forms of knowledge. It is essential to proceed from the cube as a whole. In this way the conception of the whole, of unity, stamps itself upon the child's mind, and the evolution of the particular, partial and manifold, from unity is illustrated.

---

* Forebel means that whereas in presenting the gift he has begun with forms of knowledge, the true point of departure for children must always be the forms of life.

If, now, the box is packed, as above described, so that the divided component cubes lie beneath on the bottom of it, it is only necessary for the child at the beginning of the play to reverse the box, draw away the cover, raise the box vertically and take it away, and the cube stands in complete order before the child. The object may be brought near to the life of the child by the words: A *table*—a table; a *house*—a house; or whatever else the imagination compares it to or will see in it.

From this an *armchair* or a seat can be immediately made; it is necessary merely to place the row of halved cubes upon the row of undivided cubes; this gives the back; the cubes divided in quarters can then be easily separated, and each two quarters placed together in a little four-sided column for arms on both sides, three columns to each side. This chair can be again easily changed into a *divan* (seat of repose), and this again into a *sofa*. From this is then soon formed another *armchair* with half oblique back and arms, and footbench, from which can be easily made a *bedstead*, a *child's bed*, etc.

Proceeding again from the cube, a large *business table* may be represented; from this two different *sideboards*, a *writing table*, with a *chair*, and a *basket* for *paper*. Although his representations are not before him at one time, yet the child can comprise them all in rhyme, bring them before himself in perception and remembrance, and so survey them as a whole; for example:

See how many a pretty thing
I always from the cube can bring:
Chair and sofa, bench and table,
Desk to write at when I'm able,
All the household furniture,
Even baby's bed, I'm sure;
Not a few such things I see;
Stove and sideboard here can be.
Many things, both old and new,
My dear cube brings into view;
So my cube much pleases me,
Because through it so much I see.
It is a little world.

Again, proceeding from the cube, we obtain one *large* and two *small travelling trunks* with arched lids; in the first an empty space of the size of one component cube.

From this, again, the course is quite simple and easy to buildings and houses, which the children especially like to make. House and room, table and bench, are usually the first thing the child represents, and he likes the former best opened with doors and windows. This is quite natural, for the child's world, from the remembrance of which come his formations and his conceptions, is at first principally confined to house and room, table, bench, and bed.

The child's life moves from the house and its living-rooms, through kitchen and cellar,* through yard and garden, to the wider space and activity of street and market, and this expansion of life is clearly reflected in the order and development of his productions.

House stairs, and *outside steps, wells, church, public hall*, the whole *village* with its *principal buildings*, then again the *public oven* alone, the *market place*, and here again the *townhall* or the *guardhouse*, the *city gate*, and, going out through this, the *bridge* appears. It may be seen from this how intimately my gifts are connected with the course of the child's inner and outer development; how they promote and illuminate this development; how the child by means of them strengthens and, as it were, grows out of himself. His representations proceed from his nearest experiences, and are intimately connected with them. The child is not forcibly torn away for his inner world and from his environment. But the mother or kindergartner has many opportunities of correcting the child's perceptions by his representations; and the amendments will be gladly accepted by the child if only they lie within the circle of his experiences and ideas. As these building gifts afford a means of clearing the perception of the child, they give occasion for extending these perceptions, and for representing in their essential parts, objects of which the child has only heard, as was the case in the above representations. Instructive and elevating explanations and stories, forming mind and heart, can be joined with these representations of the children, and experience has shown that children, are then doubly attentive; it seems as if the story made more impression on the child when referring to his own work.

Children of five years of age, who have gone through with similar exercises with the previous gifts, can build in common at the same time. For example:

Lay four times two whole cubes in an oblong before you; place perpendicularly upon them again four times two whole cubes. Over each two cubes lay two half cubes, so that they touch in the middle by their sharp edges; with the last two cubes, each of the two half cubes yet required is represented by two quarters. In the long hollow thus made sink four whole cubes. What have you made which now stands before each of you? "A house with an overhanging roof, four cubes high and two cubes broad."

What have each of you still left? "A whole cube and two cubes each divided into quarters."

Place the one whole cube by the right gable exactly in the middle of the wall.

Place one of the cubes, divided into quarter, in the same way, in the middle of the left gable wall.

Divide the quartered cube into two halves, and lay each of these halves in roof form on each of the two cubes so that the two small roofs shall slope in the same direction as the large roof. What have you now? "Two little outbuildings to the right and left of the house." "A large house with two little outbuildings, one on each side, each of the size of one cube, with an overhanging roof of a half cube." Can you, each of you, now build this alone? "Yes! yes!" Well, then, do it.

This play also gives great pleasure. This pleasure, as well as the principal characteristics of his product, can also be expressed by the child in song:

A house, a house, a house!
A house belongs to me.
A house, a house, a house!
Come here, come here and see!
In length it is four cubes,
In breadth it is two cubes;

In this house one has no fear.
Room, in grief and joy, is here
It is two cubes high;
A broad roof here I spy.
For smaller matters stand
Two houses at each hand.

In order further to exercise the child's power of memory and conception, all the space in the house may be filled with things with which the child is familiar; for example, here is the sitting-room, here the kitchen, etc.

A quite peculiar kind of architecture which the children like very much is that which is designated by the name of *art building*; the forms originate especially in a separation and grouping of the parts determined by symmetry and proportion, principally in vertical mural surface extension, but also in erections having in both horizontal and vertical extension at the same time; these erections receive, then , predominantly the character and expression of the columnar and monumental.

The Picture Form, or Forms of Beauty

These forms of beauty may, however, also be produced by proceeding from certain forms of life and architectural forms—e.g., from a four-sided well, or from a square table with ornaments and four cushioned seats.

With these forms of beauty it is above all important that they be developed one from another. Each form in the series should be a modification or transformation of its predecessor. No form should be entirely destroyed. It is also essential that the series should be developed so that each step should show either an evaluation into greater manifoldness and variety, or a return to greater simplicity. These points have been already discussed in connection with the forms of life, and also in the chapter devoted to the consideration of the third and fourth gifts.

We may either let the child proceed voluntarily to these forms from any chosen form of life, or we may make the series of picture forms proceed from a fixed and simple starting point. Before, however, carrying out the latter course the following fact should be considered:

The fifth gift is a cube of three times three times three, and contains twenty-seven component cubes. Therefore either the equilateral triangular form or the square form can be represented by it. Thus all the forms of beauty of the fifth gift are essentially different from those of the third and fourth gifts in this, that they separate themselves into two great distinct series:

The series of *squares* and the series of *triangles*.

The surest foundation of both, as series of cultivation and development, is found in the *forms of knowledge*. This foundation of the first series is found in that form of knowledge in which the cube is divided into *four* prisms (whose bases are isosceles triangles, each of which is composed of four and a half component cubes), and *one* square prism or tablet of nine cubes, around which the four triangular prisms are arranged in a square form.

The *second* series of forms of beauty (the triangular forms), on the contrary, find their best foundation in that form of knowledge in which the cube is divided from right to left into three equal beam-shaped parts. These parts are easily put together, so as to inclose an equilateral triangle. Each of the sides of the enclosure is nine cubes long.

We contemplate here, first of all, a series of forms of beauty which can be developed from the fundamental form of the square.

The essential beauty and the developing and forming influence of these plays, for which the greatest freedom is always given in respect to the choice of the starting point, consist in the fact that when a way of formation and development, a way of representation, is once entered upon, and we wish to come to a definite, clear aim in a definite, clear manner, we must always proceed in accordance with the chosen way till we attain to the ultimate aim of development. This course of development, everywhere perceptible in these plays, express itself here with special clearness.

In the second place, it is important that each line of development entered upon be clearly, sharply, and exactly apprehended both by ourselves and by the playing child.

Perception must clear, use and adaptation exact, and the words in which our procedure is described specific. This manner of carrying out the play is of every possible advantage, not only in its influence in the culture of the child's intellect, heart, and practical efficiency, but also in its power of creating a trustful relationship between the nurturer and the nurtured, mother and child, kindergartner and pupil. Such a trustful relationship is kept intact by an easily comprehend interchange of thought and act.

So in the case before us, especially with the execution of the first series of the forms of beauty proceeding from the square.

Inner and outer are pure opposites; therefore it may be left to the playing child himself to begin his changes from the square prism in the middle, or from the four triangular prisms outside. Inner and outer appear also in each of these two cases as opposites; and so the playing child may begin his play either in the middle of the square prism or in its outer cubes; either with the inner or outer sides of the triangular prism.

A still further choices is whether the movement shall be on all sides (that is, on four sides), or on two and two. Each beginning requires a specific development, as a certain limitation is always implied in so much change and freedom. Of course, each series of development may be broken off at any stage, and a new one entered upon, but then the playing child should himself (in the stated manner, although not by words, yet clearly, according to the object and the perception) give an account of the connected ways of formation through which the accomplished form has resulted.

We will now proceed from the fundamental form. This form, though simple, bears a great variety within itself and renders a yet greater one possible. The way of formation is that of unfolding from the middle on all sides.

Firstly, therefore, the four cubes *a* in the corners of the square prism are moved outward in a straight direction to the point where they are, as it were, fixed fast. Now, the four cubes *b* move in the same way to the four sides of the square; these together, when accomplished give the form.

If this way of development is further continued, this gives again the outward appearance, although represented by wholly different cubes or members—that is, where the cube or member *a* stood before, the cube or member *b* now stands, and where *b* stoods *a* now stands. The position of the cubes has thus wholly changed, notwithstanding the outward appearance is the same.

This change in the members of a whole, while the whole itself remains the same, is a fact of great importance for the child to observe. It is a law of Nature and of life, and one which must be recognized in studying Nature and life. Hence in the course of our plays it shall be frequently referred to, though only in the way of cursory suggestion. Other important laws of Nature and development will be dealt with in the same way—e.g., the law that the course of development may be different, but its point of departure must always be either from within, from without, or from that which mediates inner and outer.

The four cubes *a* now return to their places, the four cubes *b* remain, as it were, firmly fixed at the corners; this gives the first part of the form.

Now the developments begin in the four triangular prisms, in the middle of the longer sides (which are turned inward), and with the half cubes each of which is again divided into two parts or quarters.

But now they may themselves separate, and, as it were, one half be attracted by the middle, one half by the outside. But at the same time a development may proceed in the right-angled corners of the triangular prism, so that the outside corner cube *b*, with the one already standing at the corner, may touch the two whole cubes of the central prism by their edges.

With these ways of formation, the precise aims and final form toward which the whole course of development works, should be kept in mind, so that at last the whole appears as a purely encircling form, or as a rectangular ray-form, or as a wheel-form, connecting the two.

Each of these conceptions, again, admits of a double manner of representation, and the *environing forms* may be either a *circle* or a *square*; the *crossing rays* may be either in *right* or *oblique* position, and the same may be said of the connection of both.

Be it here remarked, in respect to all forms of beauty developed both from the square or the triangular prism, that it is essentially good if they be brought before the playing child for quiet, clear, thoughtful consideration, even if this be actually only through the relations of number. Thus we may proceed from a corner, which we touch with the fingers, accompanying the act with words as follows:

> Two and four and one and three.

Or, while contemplating the circle form:

> Two and two and two and two,
> Four and four and four and four,
> One and one and one and one,
> Three and three, three and three more!

Or—

> Four times two,
> Four times four,
> Four times one,
> and
> Four times three!

The fact remains to be brought out that very beautiful forms of connection show themselves between the forms of beauty from the square prism and the forms of life or architectural forms; these are the forms used in fortification.

We now turn to the triangular forms of beauty.

As the starting point, it appears here best and simplest to proceed from a triangular enclosure, each side of which is bounded by *nine* part cubes, and then fix upon the condition of advancement, viz., that the triangle remains the fundamental form of each newly developed figure; but that, in order to attain at the same time greater change and greater variety, one cube more at each change is by degrees set free for voluntary movement; so that the first boundary from contains on each of its sides *nine*, the second *eight*, the third *seven* of our component cubes, etc., and in the second case *one*, in the third *two* component cubes, or their parts, are destined for alternating movement.

Since each side, according to the stated limitation, must contain this number, so here no other alteration can be further undertaken than *shifting* the cubes *inside* the series, either toward the inside or outside, yet only so that the direct coherence with in the sides and among the cubes be not thereby broken up; thus that the pushed-out cube be pushed out of a certain part (one-fourth, one-half, three-fourths, etc.) of the one side, but always so that side remain connected with side. Each side of the original form, which at first was straight, may now appear as a broken line, or as a serpentine line bending in and out at one side or at the other, or as a wholly curved line, bending either inward or outward.

Simple as this alteration appears, it yet yields very manifold forms, and pleases the child just on account of the ease with which it can be accomplished.

Now a cube is set free for play, that is, for movement. What different positions may this one cube take?

It may move either inside or outside of the inclosing cubes.

In each of these two cases, again, it may be placed either in the angle (on the corner) or at the side; and here, again, either with the side or with and edge turned toward the side or the angle (corner) of the inclosing line of cubes.

There are thus given six different forms, which, however, in the series of their representation yield a logical whole, so that the child gains practice in seeking for logical members.

Further, these three free cubes may *combine* in the center of the triangle, and here, again, in a threefold manner: either always with an edge, or always with a side of each turned toward the other; or, thirdly in connection, so that the edge of the one cube is always turned toward and touches the side of the other. In the first case, three edges touch in the center; in the second case, each two edges, and this three times.

Here, again, is rendered prominent the law so highly important for life, and therefore so manifoldly expressed in nature, and hence, also, in my series of gifts—the law, viz., that in nature and in life a third connecting appearance always shows itself between two purely opposite appearances. This phenomenon was pointed out as essential even with the forms of beauty of the third gift, and on account of its deep significance we shall often return to it in the course of our demonstration.

Yet the alterations which are possible with a triangular form, one side of which contains eight component cubes, thus leaving one cube for free play, are by no means exhausted by what has been now brought forward. This whole component cube may again be diagonally divided into two equal parts, or, otherwise expressed, instead of playing with one whole cube the child may be permitted to play with two half cubes in the stated division. To give here all the alterations which are possible in this case would be impracticable, easy as they are in the execution.

The principal alterations may be: First, the two halves are divided; then, again, combined to form a prism whose are a right-angled triangle.

In the first case, not only may all the combinations above given with one cube be carried out—for example, so that both stand either on the side of line of inclosing cubes, or in the angle where two lines meet, and here, again, placed toward the outside or toward the inside; but these positions may also be manifoldly connected; for instance, one outside, one inside; one at the side and one in the angle or at the corner.

In the second case, where the two halves appear as triangular prisms, at least all the combinations take place which have already been given above with one cube, so that it is easy to suppose, and by calculation approximately find, that about one hundred combinations, or rather different representations, are possible by means of the cube divided into halves. And we are still a great distance from the end. One of the half cubes may be again divided into two quarters, so that thus the alterable members are three: one half and two quarters for each side. What a multitude of connections and alterations are given by these three members, only at *one side* and only in *one direction*! The total number of representations beginning with these three members, according to a general estimate, may amount to nearly three hundred. Notwithstanding, we are not yet at an end with the representations by means of one cube; for the second half cube may be replaced by two more quarters, so that thus four quarters are free to move. Let us here, again, assume as possible only five hundred new alterations, which is certainly not too much in proportion to the former ones; then with the triangle, where eight part cubes are on each side and one part cube either undivided or in two halves, or in one half and two quarters, or in four quarters, is free for alternate transposition, nearly one thousand representations are possible.

It may easily be seen from this how necessary it is to separate and classify the number of possible representations, so that the child may not be oppressed, or at least wearied, by their multitude. A want of classification is the bane of all the combination plays for children which have till now been known to me, and the said plays lose by this their formative influence for spirit and mind, as well as their applicability for life. But here each limitation made excludes a countless number of forms, and the child and kindergartner easily find their way amid the manifoldness of possible forms, and define the place where they stand. This may at least be done by the guide who is a true guide in virtue of ability to make such limitation and discrimination. Thus these plays are not oppressive an wearying, do not lead into unfathomable depths, but, on the contrary, are truly strengthening and developing. The educator at least always knows where he is at home, whence the child proceeds, whether his direction tends, and to what side he turns.

As in the preceding series there were always eight cubes remaining in each side of the inclosing form, so in the next there must be but seven ; thus *two* cubes are free for play. These two may now be either both undivided, or one cube undivided, the other divided; and, again, either into two halves, or into one half and two quarters; or into four quarters. Or both cubes are divided either into four halves, or into three halves and two quarters; or into two halves and four quarters;

or into one half and six quarters; or into eight quarters.

Whoever has attentively followed the course of play up to this point will be aware of the great number of possible representations, and will realize how essential to the welfare of the child it is to restrict the freedom of change by limiting it to fixed members and be determining it to a definite direction and goal.

It is evident that with all the representations indicated may be connected a movement in the environing cubes. This form of change has purposely been omitted, in order not to bewilder the imagination with too much variety. These pushings in and out may, however, be carried out practically with the different representations, and will give to the play an entirely new charm.

The smaller the number of the cubes which must remain in one side of the fundamental form, the more numerous in parts and the richer in structure become the representations. The individual parts as well as the whole also tend toward the curved form.

From this point the progress can be easily made to two and two sided forms, rectangular as well as curved, and from these to the circle as the conclusion of the whole series of representations.

From these forms approximating to the circle there is an easy transition to the representation of the different kinds of cog-wheels, and hence to a crude preliminary idea of mechanics.

Mediational between the triangular forms of beauty and the forms of life are the representations of intrenchments, sconces, and redoubts. Allusion has been made to forms of this kind in connection with the transitions from forms of beauty based upon the square and forms of life.

As the outcome of the representations indicated it is clear that in forms made with the fifth gift there rules a living spirit of unity. Even members and directions which are apparently isolated are discovered to be related by significant connecting members and links, and the whole shows itself in all its parts as one and living—therefore also a life-rousing, life-nurturing, and life developing totality.

In conclusion, just a single word with regard to the use of the lithographed leaves.

These leaves are intended originally and predominantly for parents and kindergartners, and their object is to help the person who is to guide the child's play to a comprehensive view of the gift as a whole, in order that she may intelligently follow the indications given by the children, and may be able to show to the latter the meaning of their own productions, and the connection of these productions with their life, its moving impulse and its demands.

Later, when the children have discovered and made several, or indeed most, of the things represented by the plates, or at least similar ones, then the diagrams representing the things they have themselves formed may be shown to them for imitation. This serves several purposes: it gives them a picture of what they have already represented and may again represent like the picture; it makes their insight into the whole more clear, and it extends their survey; finally, it develops their power of thought, makes their conceptions richer and more definite, and their representations of these conceptions more sure and fixed. Thus it awakens in them the power and desire to increase such conceptions by the contemplation of sculpture and pictures, whenever they have an opportunity.

8

Movement Plays for Children

In every activity and deed of man—yes, even in every activity of the smallest child—is expressed a relationship. Each act attempts to promote some end or to represent some idea. To realize his aims, man, and more particularly the child, requires a material (a substantial particular means, though it be only a bit of wood, or a pebble) with which he makes something or which makes something or which he makes into something. In order to lead the child to the handling of material, we gave him the ball; the sphere which develops from it; the cube and the other bodies discussed in the chapters relating to the kindergarten gifts. Each of these gifts incites the child to free self-activity, to independent movement. Up to the present, however, no special consideration has been given to the movement plays which develops from the gifts. This omission has been deliberate, and has been in the spirit of my general method of development and nurture—a method which descends from the universal to the particular, from the whole to the part, from unity the diversity. Now, however, that we have reached a determinate point in the consideration of those plays which require a given material, it is well that we should also give our attention to the pure movement plays. It would have been preferable, before discussing the movement plays, to explain the sixth gift (the cube divided into twenty-seven bricks, three of which are divided lengthwise, and six of which are divided crosswise into square prisms); but in this case it would have been necessary to postpone too indefinitely my answer to the appeals which flow in form all sides with reference to the kindergarten games. To these games I shall now exclusively confine myself.

For the nurture and development of childhood it is by no means sufficient to respond through play material to the external manifestations of unfolding power. We must spy out the inner process and method of development and meet the needs indicated thereby.

All outer activity of the child has its final ground in his inmost nature and life. The deepest craving of this inner life, this inner activity, is to behold itself mirrored in some external object. In and through such reflection the child learns to know his own activity, its essence, direction, and aim, and learns also to order and determine his activity in correspondence with the outward phenomena. Such mirroring of the inner life, such making of the inner life objective, is essential, for through it the child comes to self-consciousness, and learns to order, determine, and master himself. The child must perceive and grasp his own life in an objective manifestation before he can perceive and grasp it in himself. This law of development, prescribed by Nature and by the essential character of the child, must always be respected and obeyed by the true educator. Its recognition is the aim of my gifts and games apprehended relatively to the educator.

The external phenomena in the active life of the child must not be considered externally and isolatedly by the educator. They must always be studied in their relation to the inner life, either as proceeding from it or in their recoil upon it. The children themselves will be our guides and teachers in this twofold consideration. The smallest child moves joyfully, springs gayly, hops up and down, or beats with his arms when he sees a moving object. This is certainly not merely delight in the movement of the object before him, but it is the working of the inner activity wakened in him by the sight of outer activity. Through such vision the inner life has been freed. Furthermore, observation even of very small children shows that they do not rest contented in the moving object, but seek to find out whence the movement proceeds. Similar should be the procedure of the educator with reference to objects in movement (movement perhaps called forth by the child's own activity). In the nurture, development, and education of the child, and especially in the effort to capacitate him for action, his own nature, life, energy, must be the main consideration. The knowledge of isolated and external phenomena may occasionally be a guidepost pointing our direction, but it can never be a path leading to the specific aim of child culture and education; for the condition of child education is none other than comprehension of the whole nature and essence of humanity as manifested in the child, and the most complete possible realization and representation of the same, from the first appearance of the man as child and throughout the whole course of life. No education which fails to hold this aim consciously and persistently in view can, strictly speaking, claim to be an education worthy the nature of man.

After this introductory preface we consider the movement plays, their starting point, and their course of development.

Starting Point and Course of Development of the Movement Plays

The child, although unconsciously, strives to make his inner life outwardly objective, and thus perceptible, and so to become conscious of it, to see it mirrored in the outward phenomena. It is for this reason that the child tries to do himself whatever he sees done.

The ball may now be set in motion, either by the activity of the child or that of the mother.

Let it, therefore,

Its power to prove,
Stir and move,
Go and come,
Roll and run,
Hop and Spring,
Turn and swing,
Go low, then high,
In circle fly,
Go far, come nigh.
From one place to another then
The little ball can roam again.

But it can also hide itself,
To tease the little one;
Away into the dark can go,
Or fly toward the sun.

All this the little child can learn,
Can gladly in the ball discern,
And learn to trust his strength in turn.
What rich, what active life and thought
The ball to this young child has brought!
The life in both but one life stays,
Though it so many forms displays.

In these activities of the ball, which in reality and practice yield more variety than is here indicated, the whole of the movement plays are contained as in a germ. The manner of their development is also in some degree implied, or shown, as it were, in a rough sketch.

As the ball stirs, moves, goes, run, and rolls, the child who is playing with it begins to feel the desire to do likewise. Thus the little game, "The child wants to go, too!" was actually born of the incitement of the ball-plays.

Each sure and independent movement, either of his whole body or of one of his limbs, gives the child pleasure because of the feeling of power which it arouses in him. Even simple walking produces this effect, for it gives the child a threefold feeling, a threefold consciousness: First, the consciousness that he *moves* himself; second, that he moves himself from one place to another; third, that through this movement he attains or reaches something.

If, therefore, we desire to work beneficently upon the future activity of a child, if we wish to give a solid foundation to his later doing and creating, we must carefully observe and foster his earliest activities, his earliest movements, his first walking.

It is a well-established fact that his first walking gives the child pleasure as an expression of his power. To this pleasure, however, are soon added the two joy-bringing perceptions of thus coming to something, and of being able to attain something. These several perceptions should all be fostered at the same time. Care should be taken that the child use his whole power even in his earliest walking. He should move securely, firmly, and in an orderly manner. In other words, he should get his limbs, and indeed his whole body, into his own power. He should learn to use his bodily strength and the activity of his limbs for definite purposes. The careful guidance of the child in these respects is important for his whole future life, and undoubtedly the very first manifestations of the child in his own attempts at walking point to the threefold consciousness and purpose indicated. Thus, when holding by the hand or finger of mother or nurse, the child makes his first attempts at walking he frequently tries go to some particular object (often, too, he will avoid some particular object in order not to be impeded in his walking). The effort to reach a particular object may have its source in the child's desire to hold himself firm and upright by means of it, but we also observe that it gives him pleasure to be actually near the object, to touch it, to feel it, to grasp it, and perhaps also—which is a new phase of activity—to be able to move it. Hence we see that the child, when he has reached the desired object, hops up and down before it, and beats on it with his little arms and hands, in order, as it were, to assure himself of the reality of the object and to notice its qualities.

It is well, while the child is making these experiments, to name the object—e.g.; There is the chair, the table, the bench, the flower, the sister, etc.

In like manner it is well to name the parts of the object—e.g.: This is, or here is, the seat; here is the leg; here is the corner; here is the edge, etc. Its properties may also be named: The chair is hard or soft; the seat is smooth; the corner is pointed; the edge is sharp. The object of giving these names is not primarily the development of the child's power of speech, but to assist his comprehension of the object, its parts and its properties, by defining his sense-impressions. Through a rich store of such experiences the capacity for speech will of necessity be developed. Language will, in accord with the nature of spirit, break forth of itself through the augmentation of spiritual self-activity.

In order to help the child to this store of rich experiences it is well, from the time that he begins to walk, to accustom him to raise himself to his feet by the help of different objects, and also to incite him to go around such objects. Each new phenomenon is a discovery in the child's small and yet rich world—e.g., one may go round the chair; one may stand before it, behind it, beside it, but one can not go behind the bench or the wall.

Proceeding in this way, the nurture of the child ceases to be a task performed thoughtlessly and tediously, and becomes a duty which arouses and nourishes the spirit, and satisfies the inner nature. When these truths are understood, the noble and blessed calling of a true nurse will be entered upon not form motives of cold external obligation, but for the satisfaction and fulfilment of the craving for a higher degree of inward life.

The smallest child who begins to exercise the power of walking loves to go from place to place—i.e., he likes to turn about and to change the relationships in which he stands to different objects, and in which they stand to him. Through these changes he seeks self-recognition and self-comprehension, as well as recognition of the different objects which surround him, and recognition of his environment as a whole. Each little walk is a tour of discovery; each object is an America—a new world, which he either goes around to see if it be as island, or whose coast the follows to discover if it be a continent.

After this apparent digression, which is, however, in reality not a digression but a penetration into the heart of our subject, let us return to our movement plays, and especially to our first movement play, "The child wants to go on a journey"; recognizing therein the point of departure for a new and distinctive series of games—viz.:

A. The Travelling of Journeying Plays

The significance, spirit, and aim of these plays we have already recognized. They are plays whose object is to exercise and develop the child's power of independent movement. They are journeys of discovery. They are plays which enrich the child perceptions and experiences.

1. The Child wants to Travel, or Go About.

For this play the children stand in a circle; the ball has just moved from one child to another, and has thus called forth the desire for locomotion in the child. I might say that one can feel this in the children, even in one particular child. Remarking this, let the wandering of the ball cease, and, while drawing the child by the hand into the middle of the circle, express the observation just made, "Lina [or Adolph, for example] wishes also to walk about."

Or if the kindergartner perceives that the wandering of the ball no longer enchains the attention of the children, let her awaken the slumbering inclination of the children by the question, "Will not one of you also walk about?" We have never yet asked this question that several children have not at the same time stepped forth and called out, "I," "I," "I."

The leader now sings to the play-circle:

Our Lina [Adolph] likes to walk
From one place [child] to another.

Or from the heart and lips of the child itself come the words:

I, too, would like to walk, etc.

While the child who desires to walk steps up to any one in the circle, reaches his hand to that one and moves relatively to himself from the right to the left, but relatively to the circle of children from the left to the right hand; the children sing:

Our Lina [Adolph] you see will walk
From one place [child] to another.

As the walking child holds out the right hand, each child in the circle responds by extending the right hands toward him.

Smaller children can, at the first, be permitted to go round merely with this silent offering of the hand; but the next time, or even at once with larger children, the greeting may be added:

And wish you a good day, good day,
Good day, good day, good day.

Or the song proceeds from the children in the circle:

And wish us a good day, good day, etc.

The walking child, moving on, reaches his right hand to another child, and says "Good day" at the same time. The greeted child in the circle does the same.

The children play this game very willingly. When one child has ended his walking, several more always step forward who wish to "walk" in the same way. It is, of course, understood that the leader must see that *all* the children have walked at the close of the play.

An extension of this play may be added at the close of the walking of each child, by asking the child, who has again placed himself in the middle:

"Whom have you then learned to know on your journey?"

As an answer to this, the child must mention the names of the children standing in the circle. This brings about a double exercise: it teaches him not to pass by objects without observing them, and also helps him to form a definite conception of the name of the object and its qualities, or at least its general impression. A third exercise may be added to this, viz., older children may be required to name their companions in the exact *order* in which they were greeted. This is a very beneficial exercise, as it links memory and *perception*; it also exercises the power of grasping objects in a series and of the holding in mind their arrangement and sequence.

Very young children may be permitted at first to point with one finger to each child as he is named (the named "pointing" finger receives thus its true significance). Older children should merely follow with their eyes the order of the children standing on the circle. The still more developed child should be able to name the children standing on the circle in proper order, even when his back is turned toward them. Finally, when the child has gained a degree of intellectual power, he should be asked to close his eyes and name his comrades on the circle in their proper order, and, if he has as unusually vigorous and active mind, he may even mention their names in reverse order.

These hints are sufficient to show that the walking game admits of a progressive development running parallel with the development of the child's intellectual power. It admits also of a progressive external development, for, as the child gains power of walking longer, the children on the circle can step farther apart and thus increase its size.

Instead of arranging themselves in a circle, the children may form a square or rectangle, if the shape of the playroom permits.

I purposely recur to the possibility of development which lies in the simplest of the plays suggested by me; for through this capacity for development they meet the requirement insisted upon, that each new and separate play should develop from those already given. This quality of continuous evolution in correspondence with the unfolding of the child gives a quite peculiar value to my plays and my method playing.

Following the genetic idea of the walking game, our next development and extension of the play must be the walking of all the children at once. This development came itself in the playroom, unfolding naturally from the children and the game.

It is natural (i.e., it lies wholly in the nature of the object an in the nature of the child) that the wandering of the individual should awaken the impulse of wandering in all, and should inspire the desire of wandering together. Thus, in actual experience, the general wandering or traveling game arose as a spontaneous and yet necessary development, just as leaves and blossoms develop from the bud.

2. The General Travelling Game

The children are standing side by side on the circle. The magical question of the leader, "Would you *all* like to go on a journey?" raises into consciousness, or at least into articulate feeling, the wish that slumbers in each heart, and the children arrange themselves easily by twos in a line. The leader gives expression to the wish stirring in all, in the form of a song, the words of which she repeats while walking around the room. The words are learned with unconscious quickness by the children, because expressive of their own life. When learned, leader and children sing in concert:

We all like well to walk about
From one place to another;
This walking suits us well to-day,
For all things in the world look gay.
Walking, walking, walking.

I have described the blossoming of this play out of the life of the children just as it actually occurred. Imagine the line of wandering children moving repeatedly around the playroom, and occasionally making a change by marching on its diagonal. The words "All things in the world look gay" wakens the wish to see the gay and beautiful world, and on first spring day the shining sun beckons through the window, and the clear blue sky is seen through it, the doors open as if of themselves, they open repeatedly, and the gay garland of child-flowers goes through them into the open air, singing first with increased zest the already given words, then giving words to the new observations and perceptions for which God's free world offers occasion:

We hear the birdies singing
We hear their glad songs ringing;
We see the fruit trees blow;
We hear the small bees humming;
We hear the beetle [chafer] drumming;
The clouds above us go—
Let us too be going.

To pasture flocks are going;
The meadows green are growing;
And all things joy are showing;
So let us too be going!*

---

*The preceding song was composed as it proceeded from life H.Langethal to whom th words were afterwa:d communicated,took up the song, for the easier singing and comprehension of the children in regular stanzas, with a concluding extension as follows:

We all like well to wander
From one place to another;
This wander suits us well to-day,
For all things in the world look gay.
Wander, yes, wander!

We see the trees now blowing,
White clouds above us going;
We hear the birdies singing,
We hear their glad song ringing.
Wander, yes, wander!

Not merely for a change, but in order to guide the child yet more to the notice of surrounding things, to the perception of the increased feeling in his own breast, and for the fostering of human childlike feeling, the following words may also be sung:

> Journeying, travelling,
> Gives us joy too great to tell;
> Makes our breast with pleasure swell.
>
> Merry we, and safe from harm,
> With our dear ones arm in arm.
>
> Many good things now we know,
> Pretty things we've named also;
> Now a resting place choose well;
> We of all these things will tell.

According to the words of the song, when the place of rest is reached questions are asked concerning what each of the children has particularly remarked and retained in its memory, and praise is awarded to most acute observation.

But these walkings or journeys can also take place as—

3. Walking plays with a great number of children in a relatively small space, as was shown by Principal Jeckel in Frankfort-on-the-Main, suggested by our smaller walking play; where they performed a walking play in which several hundred children joined by fours, with a suitable gay some, in a spacious school garden.

Our children in Blankenburg play this game in their large playroom as well as in the open air, with great willingness and delight. I think, therefore, always with gratitude of the

---

> See flocks to pasture going!
> The meadows green are growing,
> We hear the beetles drumming,
> Bees busily are humming.
> Wander, yes, wander!
>
> The children now hear daily
> The brooklets rushing gayly;
> Where'er our footsteps lead us,
> There Nature's beauties feed us
> Wander, yes, wander!

one who made us acquainted with it, and especially who presented us with the suitable song.

But walking and journeyings are very often connected with visiting; visiting, again, is connected with social calls.

4. Visiting Play, or Going to Make Calls,

which, as will readily be perceived, is a progressive development from the walking, and embodies the same spirit.

The children stands opposite to each other, and according to their number are arranged either against two or four of the walls of the playroom.

Two of the rows, which thus stands opposite to one another, now sing:

> Those whom opposite we see
> Come to visit you and me:

and while they sing they approach each other, so that at the end of the rhyme they meet in the middle of the room.

One of the two rows, now standing closely opposite to one another, sings, while bowing to the other:

> We greet you all—we greet you all.

The second row answer:

> We thank you all—we thank you all.

The two rows now unite to form a double line, and, turning toward the play-leader, sing:

> Come, let as all go walking; we
> So many pretty things will see;
> In our stories we will tell
> What we see and love so well.

While the song is sung the column of children moves toward one corner of the room, bends there and moves along the side of the wall until opposite a second corner, then turning, walks first toward the middle of the room and next to the third corner. When this corner is reached the column bends again and moves along the second wall until the fourth corner is reached, from which point it diverges again toward the middle of the room. Here the children remain standing in their original order after having formed in their journey a figure eight in a horizontal position (∞).

The leader (or whoever else may wish to do so) now goes to each child and ask what he has seen in his journeys. The children may describe either what they have actually seen, or something that "make-believe" to have seen.

The questioner connects the different objects named by means of an impromptu story in which all bear some part. This story should both give the child pleasure and convey some helpful conception of Nature or human life.

Whenever the story-teller mentions an object which one of the children has seen, or made believe to see, during the walking in room or garden, this child must raise his hand partly as a sign that he is giving his attention to the story, and partly that the story-teller may be sure not to omit the mention of any object.

At the close of the story the travelers sing to the story-teller:

> For your story now we pay
> Hearty thanks to you to-day.

While the children sing, the double column separates into two lines which face each other. Each line then moves backward to its original place, singing:

> We now go back and take our place;
> Please turns to us again each face.

If there are four lines, or, rather, two double columns of children, the second column now begin the play. If, as has generally been the case in my experience, the children enjoy the play and wish to repeat it, they should be permitted to do so.

The sources of the children's delight in this game are manifold. The song itself is pretty; the children love to greet each other; finally, there is a fascination in the winding movement, with its varied suggestion of the relationship between center and circumference. For the same reason, perhaps—

5. The Winding Brook

was one of the first movement and traveling games developed by our circle of children, with whom, moreover, it was always a prime favorite.

The children stand side by side in a large circle. They hold each other's hands. The leader breaks the circle at a point near one corner of the room, and by a series of winding movements parallel to the shorter sides of the room leads the children first toward the inside of the circle and then outward toward the wall opposite. As the first child follows the leader, so each successive child follows his neighbor. When the winding line has thus reached the opposite narrower side, it turns, going along one of the long side back to the starting point, and this is repeated as often as the as the duration of the song requires. To this the following song is sung, partly by full chorus, partly more softly by a single voice:

Chorus: Side by side now, fast and slow,
Winding like a brook we go.
Single: By the brook the flower blow,
Gayly past them we all go.
Chorus: Side by side now, fast or slow, etc.
Single: In the watery mirror see,
Clearly showing hill and tree.
Chorus: Side by side now, fast or slow, etc.
Single: Mirrored in our hearts, too, shows
Love that toward us ever goes.
Chorus: Side by side now, fast or slow, etc.
Single: Filled with thanks and great delight
Are our hearts; our eyes are bright.
Chorus: Side by side now, fast or slow, etc.
Single: Oh, how happy are we all
Here together, large and small !
Chorus: Side by side now, fast or slow, etc.
Single: Now we turn in circle gay,
a. Singing in our childish way,
b. Singing in another way.

As the final chorus is begun, the play-leader tries to lead the merry band of children so that with the beginning of the last stanza, "Now we turn in circle gay," all the children move in a well-arranged large circle. The conclusion "*a*" is sung when the play is here ended; the conclusion *"b,"* on the contrary, when a new play is connected with it.

This brook play forms the transition from the pure journeying plays to those which through form or movement represent some object.

B. Representation Plays

One of the favorite plays which very early budded and developed in our play-circle is—

1. The Snail

The children stand, side by side and hand in hand as before, in a large circle; they also like very much to play this as a continuation of the brook, in which case the strophe *"b"* is sung at the end of the latter.

The play-leader now takes the hand of one child in the circle at any point he thinks best, breaks the circle and leads this child, whom the rest easily follow, firmly clasping each other's hands, always round the inner side of the circle till he has formed in his course a snail line, or rather a spiral line, and stands in the middle with all the children wound round him. Then, turning backward himself, and going first of all between his own and the next line of children, he tries to unwind from the inside, which is also easily done if, firstly, the children hold firmly together, and, secondly, if the snail line is not too closely wound. To this the children sing:

The Snail Song.

Hand in hand, as all can see,
Like a little snail go we;
Always nearer, always nearer;
Always closer, always closer;
Always tighter, always tighter—
Till in closest union stand
All we children, hand in hand.

At these words the play-leader should stand exactly in the middle of the circle. If the circle of children is large, the lines "Always tighter, always tighter" must be repeated until the winding is complete and the central point attained.

When the play-leader has come into the middle of the circle, he turns immediately as above described, and the following words are sung:

Hand in hand, as all can see,
Like a little snail go we;
Always farther, always farther;
Always wider, always wider;
Always looser, always looser—
From the smallest point we go,
Till the large ring we can show.

With these words all the children should again be standing in a closed circle, and the following lines may then be sung:

Gayly we each other greet,
Thus our play we now complete.

The snail game frequently and fittingly forms the conclusion of the circle plays. It is well adapted to this purpose, since it unites all the children in one whole of living activity, and finally yields the form of the circle, which is symbolic of wholeness.

As an evolution from the actual play of the children this game had its point of departure in the swinging of the ball attached to a string around the forefinger in such a way that the ball moves in a snail line, and, gradually approaching the finger, finally rests against it. It is then unwound by a reverse movement from the finger, and finally by its own recoiling activity wound again around it. In Nature the child sees the *form* of these winding line on the snail shells he so dearly loves. These visible lien interpret the words of the song, "Always nearer, always closer," also the "Always farther, always wider," and help the child in feeling to connect movement and form.

Enough has been said to show plainly the spirit and aim of these plays. Their object is to lead the child to observation and apprehension of the life that surrounds him. We suggest, in addition, a few representative movement plays which in experience proceeded freely from the inmost life and needs of very little children. Who has not noticed how children love to turn themselves around a smooth tree or pole while clasping it with one hand or clinging to it with one arm? From this practice was developed the following play. On account of the size of our playroom, a slender column stands in the middle to support the ceiling. This column exercised a magnetic attraction upon the children. One after another would rush to it, embrace it with his little arms, and swing himself around it with shouts of pleasure. As this merry play soon attracted all the children, it became necessary to introduce a certain order into it.

2. Mill Play

Six or eight children place their right hands on the smooth column and try to hold fast by it. This feat is easily accomplished in spite of the small of their hands. The left hand of each of these children is grasped by a second child, and the left hands of this second row of children by a third row, and so on, according to the number of the children and the size of the room. In this manner, proceeding from the column as center, are formed six or eight lines, each consisting of three or four children. The whole gives the effect of *rays*, or looks like the spokes of a wheel. The children should be so grouped that the members of each concentric circle are equal strength and size. The smallest children should be placed either in the first or the last row, in order that the length of stride and quickness of movement may be proportioned to their strength. If the smallest children stands in the outermost circle, and if besides the leader there are present several grown persons, each of these takes the hands of one of weaker and more delicate children, and thus determines the speed of movement, which in the beginning must of course be very slow. Even the smallest children, however, show great agility in this play; hence the speed is soon accelerated. The leader and other adults must, however, watch the children individually and collectively, and must see to it that the movement is uniform, and that the order of the children is not disturbed.

As the children move around the column, the following lines are sung:

The old mill wheel is never still
If strongly the clear water flows;
And our mill wheel turns with a will
The way that our own pleasure shows.

In this song the whole figure produced by the children is represented as the wheel of a water mill, and the child is led to the perception of the moving power in himself and in the water, and to a comparison of these powers—i.e., of the desire which impels his own activity, and the force of the water which turns the mill wheel.

In Mr. Hochstädter's kindergarten, at Frankfort-on-the-Main, the whole was looked on as the wings of a windmill, and the first four verses of the following song were adapted to it, to which the four lines here following were added:

See the windmill how it foes!
As the wind so strongly blows,
Always round it turns; it will
Never idly stand quite still.
Our strong wind is our own fun,
So we swiftly, swiftly run.
Quickly thus the time goes by;
Oh, how happy now am I!

Our children like very much to sing this song also on account of its appropriateness. The comparison of the power of Nature and of the mind, and the interpretation of the one by the other, go through this play also.

In this same kindergarten at Frankfort the following verses were afterward added, from the children's perceptions of life:

Quickly sails the ship along,
Driven by the winds so strong.
If a stormy wind should blow,
Then aground the ship might go.

This closing of the play is also appropriate, because it leads the child's attention to the disturbing effect of a too vigorous in this play.

This game may also be played in a room without a pillar, and also in the open air. The play-leader fastens around his waist a piece of cloth or strong string, twisted several times, which is grasped by the children standing nearest, and they then turn at the same time with him. In the open air this play is particularly beautiful, if a smooth-barked, full-crowned tree is found for it.

When the movement has been executed once to the right, it is also carried out by turning to the left. (For a change, and in consideration of the small children, the short triple step may be taken instead of the longer stride).

3. The Wheel

Four, five, or six children, with their faces turned toward the middle of the circle, take each other's hands. At the place where two of the children, thus standing in a circle, have joined hands, another steps up from the other side, who grasps their joined hands with one of his and stretches the other outward like a ray. A second child like manner grasps the hand of this child, so that in this way a four, five, or six rayed star results. Each two of these rays are now again connected in a tangential direction by two children who have taken hands, so that in this way a larger circle results, like the first and parallel with it. If there are many children, this can be repeated as often as the number of the children permits. When the wheel is thus enclosed, the movement begins toward the side to which the faces of the children forming the rays or spoken are turned. To this is sung:

> See here a wheel we make,
> Which turns itself around;
> The spokes must all be straight,
> And by the fellows bound.

Principal Jeckel calls this play a star game, and has carried it out with a very large number of children in the spacious garden belonging to his school.

It is very evident, as has already been mentioned, that through these plays, and the free and joyous self-expression which they involve, the child is led to observe both surrounding objects and the phenomena of his own life; that through such observation he is further led to comparison and recognition of the two orders of phenomena, and, finally, to healthful and salutary judgements and inferences. The pleasure with which the children play these games, and others of a similar kind, may therefore have its ground in a presentiment of what is symbolic and significant in them. May not their delight in these encircling movements, for example, spring from the longing and the effort to get an all-round or all-sided grasp of an object?

Through many considerations, and as the result of many and various experiences, I am convinced that the exalted and often ecstatic delight of children in their simple movement plays is by no means to be explained through the exertion of mere physical force—more bodily activity. The true source of their joy is the dim premonition which stirs their sensitive hearts (*Gemüthe*) that in their play there is hidden a deep significance; that it is, in fact, the husk within which is concealed the kernel of living spiritual truth.

Hence it is that we can not too strongly insist upon the thoughtful observation of children's play—upon their nurture and development , and upon their purification from all that obscures or is foreign ti their ideal content. Through the exclusion of foreign elements the immanent ideal of the play—which is what really stirs the soul of the susceptible child—will become more powerful in its influence. I am convinced that in this way me not only arouse and illuminates the ethical feeling of the child, but also strengthen it and elevate it into practical activity; and, finally, that this practical moral activity will recoil with blessed effect upon the nurture and development of religious aspiration.

In the presentation of these plays I have purposely followed their historic genesis and evolution in our own circle of children. My object in this historic presentation has been to show how, through holding in my own mind the fundamental idea and characteristics essence of these plays, I have been enabled to follow with fostering influence the absolutely free development of the child, and to respond to the indicated needs of his being. Generalizing the results of this experience it becomes apparent that, through an education which is rooted and grounded in the nature of man, which recognize in that nature the one true point of departure for its whole procedure, it is possible to combine a fixed adhesion to the universal with the most searching and careful nurture of the particular and individual.

4. The Circle, Star, Flower and Crown Play

The children form a large circle. The leader quietly arranges it so that the more advanced children are distributed in the four quarters of this circle. These quarters (of the circle) are then pointed out by the leader, and the advanced child in each quarter is asked to watch over the development of the play in his or her quarter, and to preserve order. The whole circle moves round first to the right, afterward to the left, singing:

> Side by side now, fast or slow,
> In a large round ring we go;
> While around our circle going.
> From our lips gay songs are flowing.
> 'Tis as pleasant we soon learn,
> In the smaller rings to turn,
> And to sing out soft and gay—
> That is happy children's way.

At the conclusion of the words "'Tis as pleasant, we soon learn," the play-leader claps his hands, and each of the four quarters of the circle forms immediately a smaller circle of its own, which is closed at the words "In the smaller rings to turn"; and now each of the smaller circles turns round to the right; at the repetition of the verse "'Tis as pleasant, we soon learn," each circle turns round to the left.

Again the play-leader claps his hand. All the children in each circle stretch the right hand into the middle of the circle, reach out the left in ray form toward the outside, turn to the right, and sing:

> Now we have formed a star,
> Now we have formed a star,
> Clear shining, though so far;
> Our parents love [father, mother loves] the star.

Or, generally,

> Who does not love the star?

The play-leader claps again, all the children in each circle stretch the left hand into the middle of it, and the circle now moves to the left, singing the former song.

The play-leader clap again, each of the children in each circle lays its right arm over the left, the right hand turned inward above, the left turned inward below, so that the opposite hand may be easily grasped by two neighboring children; when this is done, the children of each circle turn round to the right and sing:

> Our flower's form complete must be,
> As those we in the garden see,
> Which with their glances bright
> The gardener delight.

Again the play-leader claps, the children lay the left hand over the right (the left turned inward above, the right below), the clasp hands, turn round to the left, and sing as before. At the conclusion of the song the play-leader claps again, the children drop each other's hands and raise their arms, the palm of the hand turned outward. Each two neighboring children lay their opposite palms firmly against one another, so that the whole forms a crown with alternating points. The children turn to the right and sing:

> Great pains we now are taking,
> Crowns for our parents making;
> We try to make them right,
> Our parents to delight.

The play-leader claps again, and the children turn to the left.

Again he claps. Each of the children lets his or her hand fall on the shoulders of his or her two neighbors. With this they turn and sing:

> We have formed a garland gay
> Which completes our little play;
> Lovingly we thus were bound
> As happily we turned around.
> Let us now, the selfsame way,
> Turn in circle large and gay;
> Clear and loud our merry singing

From the echo back is ringing.
Though both star and wreath have vanished,
From our circle none are banished

At the words "Let us now, the selfsame way," the play-leader claps, and the four circles open in the places turned toward the middle of the room. From this point each circle swings or goes backward in two opposite directions outward, so that the four smaller circles now again stand in the large circle as in the beginning of the play. Here the children standing by one another (who are as yet separate) take hands immediately, and at the words "turn in circle large and gay" the whole circle turns round to the right. After the concluding words the circle dissolves. Each child gives his right hand to his two neighbors.

These four representations—circles, star, flower, and crown—are considered and treated in a composite and connected play; but with quite small children, each may be played by itself as a single game, and several times repeated, though the intermediate children like very much to play it as a coherent whole.

The nature and spirit of this play are plain—viz., that the children are to be led by it to the observation of Nature, of their own life, of the movements of their hearts and of their childlike human feelings, and to the fostering of these as of their thoughtful child life in general.

C. The Running Plays

The child seeks to exercise his ever-increasing power of walking, and to measure his strength with that of other; the pure running plays, the outrunning and overtaking plays, are first plays, of the completely developed power of movement. The play with his ball incites the child to movement games, and gives him an opportunity to practise them. The little ball escapes from the child's hand; it runs away, and the child tries to overtake it, reach it by running after it. But the pure running plays are also developed from the play itself.

1. The Racing Game

is the prime favorite with our children. It is played in the open air, on the playground, and on the sufficiently broad garden paths, as well as in the spacious playroom.

This racing ground is a large, quadrangular course, which encloses the beds and gardens oh the children as the frame encloses a slate.

The children are arranged by twos, as nearly as possible according to equal size, strength, and dexterity.

Each pair of children step in turn before the play-leader into the course in the middle of one of the broad sides, back to back. The play-leader and the running children sing:

> Children, your limbs move now—
> Run! Your swiftness prove now.
> Run now—run now faster,
> Faster still, and faster!

At the word "run" the leader claps his hand, and the children, using all their power, run in opposite directions. At the point opposite from the starting place the runners pass each other, and each of them tries to reach first the opened arms of the play-leader.

Upon the second repetition of the race two of those who have won the prize in the former race go first into the course. Even this very simple movement game is played by the children with great pleasure.

Other running plays will be mentioned when we reach the point whence they proceed, as it were, form the life of the children with their gifts.

Hitherto the position of the body and the movement of the limbs have not been restricted, but both of these can be considered in simple walking.

D. The Pure Walking Games

Be it said, by the way, that the name *walking games* (since girls also share them) is much more appropriate than the foreign designation of "marching."

1. The Simple Walking Game

This can be done in a single row as well as in a double row by children standing in pairs; the latter is easier for the children, and they like it better.

A good deal of discretion can be used in the arrangement of the children. Either a larger child can be placed with each smaller one, or children of like size can be put together, and then again either the largest or the smallest children may be permitted to take precedence. The room, playground, or garden is then traversed in various straight and curved, circular and winding movements, to which the following words are sung:

> Step by step now let us go,
> Equal paces take also.
> Not to right nor left we turn;
> To keep the knees straight, we must learn.
> Upright must the body be,
> Head and chest and leg and knee;
> Turning out the feet must be,
> And the arms be hanging free.
> Not too near nor far away
> From his neighbor, may one stray.
> How glad are we, as two by two
> We march with measured step and true!

Or the play may be accompanied by the simple little song composed bt the before-mentioned Herr Langethal:

> We move in equal spaces,
> And all make equal paces,
> La, la, la, etc.

This walking play always gives the children great pleasure.

In changing the play and the room, the children, who are going in pairs behind one another, merely sing:

> Breast to back now, that's well; so
> To our playing let us go.

That disorder and rough disturbing willfulness may never enter, it is a good plan, whenever it is possible, to accompany each change in the play by rhyme and song; so that the latent sense of rhythm and song, and, above all, the sense of order in the human being and child, may be aroused and strengthened to an impulse for social co-operation.

With the simple walking plays may be sung simple melodies without words. Such melodies are especially adapted to the longer walks taken out of doors, when such walks over *level* paths.

2. Circular Walking Game

The walking plays, which take place around a circle, are always more difficult than those in which the movement is straightforward, because the feet have to be set sidewise. It is therefore well to practice the latter first, and to use them oftenest, especially with very small children. Nevertheless, it is noticeable that circular position and circular movement seem to have a special attraction for the smallest children. Therefore it is well to combine the two forms of play by allowing the children to move around a circle; only, instead of moving sidewise, to walk one behind the other, singing:

> Breast to back now, that's well, so;
> In the circle let us go.

In the specific circling games the children stand, not breast to back but side by side and hand in hand. When the object is to direct attention to the circle itself, the children sing:

> Merrily now, side by side,
> In a circle round we glide.

If, however attention is to be directed in part and prominently to the turning out of the feet, the children sing:

> Feet turned outward, that's fine, so;
> Gayly in a ring we go.

For the movement plays thus far considered the freely moving ball has furnished incitement and type. The ball attached to a string gives the incitement and point of departure for another series of plays. To illustrate: The children stands in the orderly circle around the leader; the leader reaches the ball (fastened to its string) to any one of the children; he himself retains firm hold of the string; he pulls the string slowly, the ball escapes from the child's hand and swings rhythmically here and there before him. The leader gives words to this phenomenon by singing:

> The little ball moves easily,
> There, here—there, here—there, here.

He now either asks the child from whose hand he lets the ball escape, "Will you also do what I have done?" or, generally, "Who will try to do as I have done?"

Usually several children come forward, and, decided by good reasons, he chooses one of them, places him in the middle of the circle of children, lets him make the swinging movement with the ball, and at the same time sing twice the above-quoted words.

The first time this game was played I noticed that the movement of the ball seemed to affect the children magnetically. As the ball moved, many of them moved also, bending first on one side, then on the other. Afterward this happened again. The movement of the children was immediately given a rhythmic form, and thus arose a whole series of movement plays proceeding from the ball, which aim at the definite training of the body and its individual members.

Movement Plays Proceeding from the Ball on the String, which have in View at the same Time an Exact Training of the Body and Limbs

A. Swinging Movement Plays

As soon as the ball, which has been swung by the child standing in the middle of the circle, has ceased to move, the general impulse of the children to move likewise is greeted by the following song:

> We too can move lightly
> Here and there, here and there.

Accompanying the song, the children move their bodies lightly from one side to other. As they sing the word "we" they rest firmly on the left foot and sightly raise the right; with the next syllable they rest upon the right foot and raise the left.

This rhythmic alteration occasions a slightly waving movement of the upper part of the body. Manifestly the rhythmic alternation may proceed from the right foot to the left, as well as from left to right, and thus produce a waving movement in a direction opposite to the one already described.

This waving movement, when continuous and uniform, not only delights the children but has a very pleasing effect, resembling a field of grain moved by the wind. It is of course understood that the leader watches the circle and sees that it is kept in good order. Each member of the circle should have a chance to lead, for it is especially developing to a child to recognize himself on the one hand in his own independent activity, and on the other as the member of a well-ordered totality.

To stand in the middle of the circle and freely swing the ball gives the children great delight, and I am firmly convinced that it is important for the welfare and development of the child that this delight should be fostered. Hence I am of the opinion that this game should be repeated often enough to allow each of the participating children to act as leader.

When the circle is a large one, however, it becomes necessary to introduce another movement to alternate with the rocking movement of the whole body. The most obvious movement which suggests itself is the swinging of the arms, and, primarily, the swinging of one arm alone, beginning naturally with the *right* arm.

Thus , when the child in the middle of the circle has swung his ball after the fashion of a pendulum, each child in the circle may swing his right arm, accompanying the movement with the words:

> My arm is lightly swinging
> Here and there, here and there.

According to the feeling of the children, either these two lines or only the last line may be repeated twice.

Instead of the words "here and there," may be sung the words "front," "back."

In order that the play may have a developing effect upon the children it is important that there should be harmony of action. Hence care must be taken that the motion of the arm is the same at each repetition of the words. Thus, with the words "front," or "back" the arm should be swung toward the center of the circle; with the word "back" or the word "there" it should be swung toward the circumference of the circle.

Only through this harmony of the word and movement can the true life and spirit of this play work and freely and effectively, and exert its fostering influence.

After repeating the movement with the right arm from four to six times, it should be carried out with the left arm, to the accompaniment of the words—

> My left arm now is swinging, etc.

Next, both arms may be swung, and this in several different ways.

First. With both arms *parallel to the sides,* and here again—*a.* Both arms may be swung at the same time and in the same direction; or, *b.* The two arms may be swung alternately and in opposite directions, to the song:

> Both arms I swing lightly,
> Front and back, front and back.

Second. Both arms may be *parallel to the breast,*, and here again—*a.* Both arms may be swung at the same time and in the same direction; or, *b.* The two arms may be swung alternately and in opposite directions.

Simultaneous movements may also be executed by the children standing with intertwined arms, around the circle.

Similar movements may be made with the legs, though they naturally admit of less variety. Thus:

The right leg here and there, or front and back; left leg moved in same manner; right leg sideways to the right; left leg sideways to the left.

For a change may be sung the words—

> Happy and successful I always shall be,
> Swinging my arms [legs] like the pendulum
> free.

Or—

My arm swings quickly to and fro,
And like the pendulum doth go.

If exercise of the hip joints seem desirable, the trunk may be moved in the same way while the lower part is held firm, singing:

I bend my body, too,
Front and back, front and back.

To make the swinging of the ball and the swinging of the arms points of departure for the perception of living Nature, and in order to give more precision to the observation of nature, the following words by Langehtal may be sung as an interpretation of the movements already described:

When they like wind-blown twigs appear,
Well pleased are then the children dear, etc.

If the number of the children is not too large, the leader may call each child singly into the circle, grasp it under the arms, and lifting it, allow the closed legs to swing to and fro while the trunk remains quiescent. Suitable words will of course accompany this exercise.

This play will be a pleasant rest for the children if they have previously been playing very active games.

When the ball is vigorously swung toward either of the two sides, it swings also wholly around itself, or in a circle around the finger tips which are holding the string fast. This circling movement of the ball on the string swung by the finger tips of the right hand now gives rise to a whole series of circling and turning child plays.

B. Circling and Turning Movement Plays Proceeding from the Ball

The child, standing in the middle of the play circle connects again with his earlier play with the ball, by singing while at the same time swinging the ball:

My little ball moves easily
There, here—there, here—there, here—
And then it swings around.

The children standing in the circle then move, rocking from one foot to the other [or, in other words, poising themselves first on one foot and then on the other], as above stated, and sing:

> And *we* like to move easily,
> There, here—there, here—there, here—
> And then we moved around.

With these latter words the whole circle goes round either to the right or left.

Each time, after all the children have turned in a circle, another child steps into the middle of the circle and swings the ball.

Just as all the children turned in a circle, so may each child turn one of its limbs in a circle. Thus the child standing in the middle can sing and show—

> My little ball, etc.
> And then it swings around.

Upon this, all the children in the circle sing:

> My *arm*, too, can, etc.,
> And then it swings around.

The arm hanging vertically can now be swung either from behind toward the front or *vice versa*.

As with the right arm, so with the left; and as with the arms, so with the legs. With the swinging of the legs the resulting circle is, of course, horizontal, as that with the swinging of the arms is vertical.

With the circling swinging of the arms may also be sung for a change:

> As the wind turns the sails of the mill,
> So my arm turns when moved by my will.

This movement may also be used as a windmill play. One of the children step into the middle of the circle, swinging its arm round, and singing:

> When fresh and strong the wind blows,
> Around with speed my mill goes.
> Through small the mill may be,
> It grinds fine meal for me.

The circle of players then turns around the child in the middle, and sing:

> Because the miller good meal made.
> Our thanks to him shall now be paid.

Another child now steps forward, and sings:

> Please let me grind as well as you,
> And then to *me* thanks will be due.

The song begins again:

> When fresh and strong the wind blows, etc.

All the children may turn their arms at the same time. To do this they must stand at a suitable distance from each other, and hence form a considerably enlarged circle. The following words may be sung:

> The mill stands high on the windmill hill;
> The strong wind blows it—it stands not still;
> The people brings the grain to the mill,
> Which grinds it to meal, the bags to fill;
> The baker bakes it—he has great skill,
> And little children eat with a will.

The many-sided developing influence of this play may be plainly seen. The final form of the game can be played as the conclusion of the whole series of exercises, and after several children have individually represented the mill.

With the circling movement of the legs and feet, the ball on the string is to be swung so that it describes a horizontal circle:

> Round and round quickly my feet I can swing,
> And, like the ball, I can make a round ring.

With the circling movement of the ball on the string (especially when played in the circle), attention may be called to the fact that one side of the ball looks toward the middle, or that it always points out the middle by its string. The child who turns the ball by the string, with constant attention to its action, sings:

> As the ball goes high and low,
> It always does the middle show.

This indication now again points to a new series of pure movement plays. All that children of the circle raise the *right* arm to a horizontal position, point with it to the middle, and, turning in a circle, sing:

Round and round now as we go,
We, pointing, do the middle show.

What was at first done with the right arm is now done with the left.

Now the children let their arms sink, turn all their faces toward the middle of the circle, turn themselves, and sing:

In a *circle* now turn we,
And always do the *middle* see.

Especial care must here be taken that the circle is a perfect one. The children will themselves notice that the more perfect the circle, the more clearly can the middle be seen and the more precisely can they point to it. This is also brought forward by the song:

If now the ring is wholly round,
The middle easily is found.

When this is clearly recognized by the playing children the leader asks: "Can say one now show me the middle? Can any one step into the middle?" A many-voiced "Yes!" will certainly follow.

The leader now begins with the child who he thinks has best understood what he has asked, and says, turning to him:

Dear one, I pray thee
The center to show me.

The leader then conducts the child as slowly as possible to the exact middle of the circle, lets him stand there a few seconds, and then leads him back, singing:

Our order you fulfilled with grace,
Now step back to your former place.

In this manner the leader conducts each child in the circle to the middle and back again. We saw this play carried out more than three years ago in several institutions with quite young children, and always to their delight. It may also be mentioned that this play was in one case spontaneously originated by the children of such an institution. Langethal, to whom this fact was communicated, has developed the play and written the following words:

> Dear one, I beg thee
> The middle to show me;
> Then we shall know
> How we should go.

If while turning in the circle there is any disorder or any deviation from the curve, etc., it is the duty of the child who stands in the middle to call attention to this deviation by raising his arm toward the side of the circle where the disorder exists. If the child fails to do this, the circle has the right to make him attend to his duty, by singing:

> Would you in the middle stay?
> You must order keep away.

This reciprocal effect of center and circumference upon each other have aroused great interest whenever the play has been repeated, and the circle has always joyfully submitted to the decision of the little leader, although small cases of disorder have been purposely incited in order to test the attention of the leader.

From this play is now developed "Child, turn thee," a play which therefore, should follow those above described, and which, just because it has by degrees proceeded from child life, is very willingly played by the children.

The children arrange themselves according to their number in three, four, and even more circles of six or at the most of eight children. Children of different sizes must stand in each circle, so that the smaller ones may be joined with the larger. The circles must be so disposed in the playroom that, considered together, they again form a whole circle.

The largest child in each circle is the leader of that circle; the general leader of all the circles stands in the middle, so that the movements in all the circles takes place simultaneously. Particular and general are beautifully brought together, and, as it were, reciprocally join hands for united and clear representation; for the very spirit and character of my plays demand that the child act with the fullest and purest demonstration of his individual life, and at the same time in accord and harmony with, in respect for and with acknowledgment of the whole and its requirements. Without fidelity to this higher spirit of play and life which can actually show itself even with ten or twelve children, the plays would lose their significance for mind and heart.

The children, arranged as described, turn and sing at the same time in the different circles at a sign from the play-leader:

> We stand here hand in hand, and sing,
> And wish to turn round in a ring;
> But first we would the middle know:
> To the child who will it show,
> Our hearty thanks shall surely go.

The child who offers himself for this position, or any child the leader chooses, is now placed exactly in the middle of the well-formed circle, and the children in the circle bow toward the middle, and sing:

> We bow to you, we bow to you,
> We bow to you,
> And while your little song you sing,
> We'll join, and move round in a ring.

The child standing in the middle claps its hand, and sings (the rest softly accompanying it):

> Around, around, in ring around, in ring
> around,
> Always around, yes, always around.

Upon this, the circle turns at the right.

At the end of the song the child claps his hands again, and the circle turns to the left, to the accompaniment of the same song.

After the conclusion of the song the child claps again, the circle stands still, and sings in chorus:

> Now, all standing still, will we
> Your smooth dancing like to see;

We to you a song will sing,
While you dance in this round ring.

The children in the circle now claps their hands and sing while the child turns exactly in the middle of the circle, and as nearly as possible upon his own axis.

From small children this spinning movement is difficult so the leader may enter the circle with the child and extend to the latter the middle finger of her right hand. Holding the leader's finger, the child easily turns like a wheel about its axle.

When the song is completed, the children standing in the circle clap their hands, whereupon the child in the center spins around, beginning toward the left instead of toward the right. The game is repeated until all the children have had the chance to spin.

The reciprocal activity of the individual and the whole circle is also marked in this game, for which reason it is a favorite for children

At the close of this whole series of games the several small circles are again merged in the one large circle from which they were previously formed. In this way the particular, the individual, and the universal are shown in gradation and harmony. Through experience of this kind of child is prepared to recognize the relationship of particular and universal in nature and in life, and finally to realize the significance of these relationships in the structure of the universe.

Among the most important experiences of life for the child, as for the adult, must be reckoned the experience that in the process of development form each given object is evolved its antithesis. The manner of this evolution is also most significant.

To enrich the child with this experiences, while he is in the age of innocence and purity, should be one chief aim of early education. This truth of evolution by antagonism should therefore be adumbrated in his plays. Later, a wise education will lift it into the region of clear consciousness and reveal it as a guiding law of life. Happy the child, happy the youth who has been led to recognize this weighty truth! The child educated in this way possesses a talisman which secures to him in his impassioned youth not only purity of life, but, what is higher, purity of mind and heart.

Such an experience we offer the children, particularly in our circling movement plays. Take for example the play "Seeing each other and not seeing each other." The children form a circle; the circle moves around. The following words (written in part by Langethal) are sung:

In circle we are winding,
La, la, la, la, la, la, la,
Each other's faces finding,
La, la, la, la, la, la, la,
Clip-a-clap, clip-a-clap.
And now the middle showing,
Yes, yes, yes, yes, yes, yes, yes,
Round which the ring is going,
Yes, yes, yes, yes, yes, yes, yes,
This is splendid—'tis fine, so
In a ring to go!

The circle now divides. The leader turns with his next playmate toward the outside and moves in the opposite direction from that before persued, this time with his back to the center of the circle—while all the players follow him hand in hand, and so by degree each turning from his place backward—close round the circle, accompanying their movements, all the children sing:

Now turning, we are winding,
The ends together binding.

According to the size of the circle, this is to be done after singing the words *once* or *twice*. As the circle is now closed, and the turning has caused all the players to stand with their faces turned outward, the leader, immediately followed by the whole circle, begins to sing:

In circle we are winding,
La, la, la, la, la, la, la,
Each other now not finding,
La, la, la, la, la, la, la,
Clip-a-clap, clip-a-clap.
We trust the middle surely,
Yes, yes, yes, yes, yes, yes, yes;
So look around securely,

Yes, yes, yes, yes, yes, yes, yes.
This is splendid—'tis fine, so
In a ring to go.

Upon this begins again, as before (but reversed), the turning of the face toward the inside, with the words:

Now, turning, we are winding,
The ends together binding.

And now the play can begin anew, as above.

In order to let the children see, as it were in a mirror, their different ways of standing, they may clap the palms of their hands together at the beginning, when the faces are turned toward one another; but later, when back is turned to back, strike the back of their hands together. Such comparisons of position, by aid of touch, are quite essential to help the child to clear insight, and must be retained whenever presented. In so far as play affords this comparison it has a developing, educating, formative influence. In the games presented by me this comparison has been employed with clear consciousness of its significance.

The game of "Seeing and not seeing each other" may, if the playroom admits, be played in a second and prettier way.

The game begin as before, with the exception that the circle is made only large enough to occupy one-half of the free space of the room (a), so that in the other half may be formed the second circle (b), wherein the children's faces are turned toward the outside. Standing in *a*, the children sing, as before:

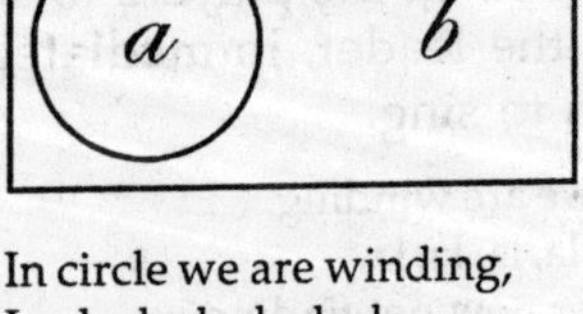

In circle we are winding,
La, la, la, la, la, la, la,
Each other's faces finding,
La, la, la, la, la, la, la,
Clip-a-clap, clip-a-clap,
And now the middle showing,

Yes, yes, yes, yes, yes, yes, yes,
Round which the ring is going,
Yes, yes, yes, yes, yes, yes, yes.
This is Splendid—'tis fine, so
In a ring to go.

The leader opens the circle toward the side *b*, where teh second half of the space is as yet free, and moves with the rest, following hand in hand, as if she would form a circle similar to the first. Turning, however, toward *b*, she moves in such a way taht with the second circle now to be formed the backs of all are turned toward the middle, and their faces toward the outside, so that the whole forms a winding line.

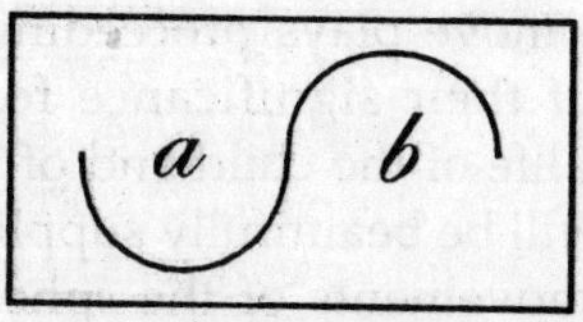

While this is going on the players sing:

Now turning, we are winding,
The ends together binding.

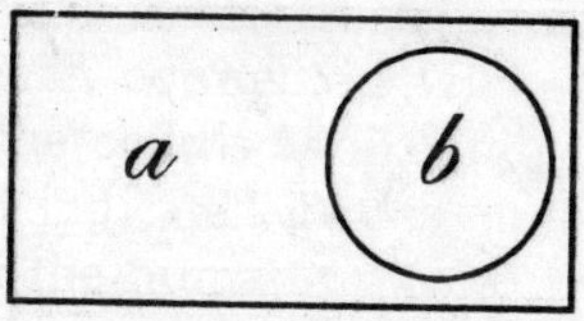

Upon this the second circle *b* is closed, with the faces turned outward in the second-half of the play-space. The circle, turning as above, then sings:

In circle wc are winding, etc.,
Each other now *not* finding, etc.;
We trust the middle surely, etc.;
So look around securely, etc.

Here also applies the previous remark about the different ways of clapping the hands.

The leader opens the circle as before, but toward the opposite side, toward *a*, and forms again a winding line in the opposite position to the first, to which the whole circle again sings:

Now turning, we are winding, etc.

The play then begins anew. The figure, therefore, which the movement of the play makes, regarded as a whole, resembles horizontal eight.

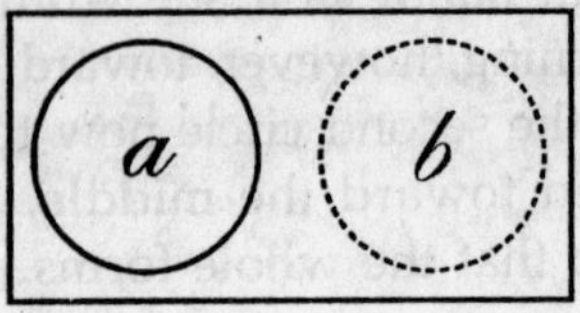

Here conclude the move plays proceeding from the ball, and the indications of their significance for the physical, intellectual, and moral life of the child and of the future man. What is omitted here will be beautifully supplied by the more definite and sharper movements of the sphere, from which the further progression of the movement plays proceeds.

Index

❑❑❑